GW00771021

HOW TO COLLECT THE MONEY YOU ARE OWED

HOW TO COLLECT THE MONEY YOU ARE OWED

MALCOLM BIRD

PIATKUS

First published in 1990 by
Judy Piatkus (Publishers) Ltd of
5 Windmill Street, London W1P 1HF

British Library Cataloguing in Publication Data

Bird, Malcolm *1932–*
 How to collect the money you are owed.
 1. Great Britain. Business firms. Debtors
 I. Title
 658.15260941

 ISBN 0–86188–977–0

Set in 11/14pt Linotron Times by
Wyvern Typesetting Ltd, Bristol
Printed and bound in Great Britain by
Mackays of Chatham plc

CONTENTS

He had lots of orders
and assets galore.
But cash was the problem:
he needed much more.
'I can't pay the bills
that's the problem you see.
Until I am paid
by the firms which owe me.'

Epitaph for a bankrupt

INTRODUCTION

IN 1989 the biggest debt collection group in Europe (Intrum) claimed that businesses in the UK were losing as much as twenty billion (yes, billion) pounds each year as a result of poor debt collection. Intrum also pointed out that UK businesses pay their suppliers, on average, 78 days after being invoiced. Such a length of time makes the notional 30-day cycle something of a nonsense. The long delay also tends to hit the small businesses hardest since they are often at the end of a chain of contractors and sub-contractors and are frequently least able to withstand the demands of *their* suppliers. Meanwhile their customers will not pay them until they in turn have been paid by *their* customers.

Overdue payments often result in the failure of small to medium-sized businesses which, living from hand to mouth, have no financial buffer to tide them over whilst waiting for money to come in.

Company liquidations resulting from insolvency have been a feature of the UK business scene throughout the 1980s with no sign of improvement. According to Department of Trade and Industry figures the average yearly number of liquidations in the years 1979–81 was 6674. The average for 1986–88 was 11,757.

The published figures for receiverships during the 1980s, whilst slightly less horrifying for the last three years of the decade, are also indicative of the cash-flow problem. The average for the years 1980–88 was 1675.

In other words, in nine years more than 15,000 companies were placed in the hands of the receiver.

These figures do not include the failures of a multitude of sole trader or partnership businesses, the vast majority of which are to be found in the small business sector.

Particularly galling for the owners of these failed businesses is a state of affairs illustrated by a comment from a banker, who said: 'The receivers often find that there is no alternative but to wind up a business despite the fact that outstanding debts are more than covered by money long overdue to the business from customers.'

How to avoid this painful situation is what this book is all about.

The emphasis is on getting the money in, but within the broad context of the whole cash-flow scene. It is not enough just to collect outstanding debts quickly – a range of financial control measures is necessary.

This broad context is also dealt with (as simply and as straightforwardly as possible) to provide a complete kit for the small to medium business to use. These ideas are not of course irrelevant in the big business. It is not unknown, for example, to find a large business financing a warehouse full of surplus finished product or raw materials.

The difference is that the big business is more likely to be able to afford it – and may finance it at least in part by delaying the payment of money due to their small suppliers!

However, the emphasis in the chapters which follow is on the technique necessary to get the money in. This includes the steps which a business must take to eliminate delays resulting from its own internal actions and arrangements as well as the way to go about obtaining payment after the money has become due.

Some legal advice is also included, but since the law can be changed (or re-interpreted) and because subtle differences in circumstances can be crucial, it is important to obtain qualified legal advice before entering into litigation. Hopefully, if the other advice is followed having recourse to the courts will not be necessary.

To avoid the cumbersome expressions 'his/hers', 'he/she', etc. the masculine form has been used throughout the book. Unless the context otherwise indicates, both genders are implied.

1

THE CASH-FLOW SCENE

- **The slide into insolvency**
- **Can your bank help?**
- **The key factor**
- **The cash-flow scene: Key Points**

THERE is a scenario familiar to thousands of businessmen the world over.

Having struggled to set up the business and make its presence known in the market the first few orders are obtained. The period of euphoria which follows is normally brief and ends abruptly when the businessman realises that he is on a merry-go-round which carries him deeper and deeper into trouble and with no apparent means to get off.

The slide into insolvency

The cycle of events goes like this:

1. Cash has been raised by means of loans secured by mortgages on home and/or business premises. In some cases unsecured loans will have been obtained from family and friends and the owner(s) of the business may have committed their personal savings.

2. A substantial sum has been spent on the legal costs of setting up the business, finding premises, advertising, finding staff, obtaining machinery, laying in basic stocks of raw materials, etc., etc., etc. By this time a significant part of the cash available to the business is likely to have been used up.

3. Orders begin to arrive and further expenditure is made to meet them. Wages are paid, fuel, power and raw materials are consumed and a variety of small items of expense incurred.

4. The first deliveries are made and invoices mailed out to the customers.

5. More orders arrive and are fed into the pipeline – at about the time that suppliers' bills start to arrive.

   Expenditure to meet the sales orders continues and indebtedness to suppliers increases.

6. Payments from customers are slow to arrive but wages still have to be paid and any delay in paying suppliers results in

dunning letters and threats to withhold further supplies until the accounts are settled.

7. In the meantime, yet more orders have arrived or are in the offing with, now, no apparent means to finance them as cash resources are fast running out.

8. The businessman approaches his bank for a loan, or an increase in loan, showing the bank manager his list of outstanding orders as evidence that the further loan is justified. The bank, which is making a fat profit from the charges associated with the initial loan, may do one or more of a number of things:

   - express sympathy
   - insist on further security before agreeing to a further loan
   - give the businessman a lecture
   - agree to a loan subject to the businessman providing monthly cash-flow forecasts, schedules of indebtedness and other data
   - offer an overdraft (at considerable cost) for a limited period
   - refuse to help in any way at all, safe in the knowledge that if the business goes bust the bank has its security in the form of mortgages on factory or other premises.

9. With perhaps some limited help in the form of overdraft or loan the businessman sets about completing his orders and eagerly scans the post each morning hoping for a cheque from a customer.

   He *will* find in his post the electricity, gas and telephone bills which *must* be paid or he will be cut off. He must also pay the wages of his employees and meet his suppliers' demands, or risk having no one to do the work and no materials to do it with.

10. Eventually, being unable to meet his debts and having received insufficient money from customers, the bank forecloses and the business goes to the wall.

3

A pessimistic scenario? Certainly, but one which is only too common.

Can your bank help?

There is a less disastrous scenario which, although less agonising, can cause the owners of the business much humiliation and frustration. This is the situation in which, in order to obtain additional funding from the bank, the businessman agrees to provide regularly to the bank manager cash-flow forecasts, lists of outstanding debtors/creditors and other means to evaluate assets and liabilities. The result is that valuable time must be spent with the bank manager (who probably has no hands-on experience of running a business like yours) while he tells you what you can and cannot do. Although, in some cases, this treatment can save an inexperienced or imprudent entrepreneur from greater catastrophe, the fact is that the business is being run by the bank and not the owners.

Another trap to avoid is that of trying to prop up a business which is fundamentally unsound (e.g. overheads are too high for the possible volume of trade) by taking on more and more loans. This is a slippery slope with, in effect, good money being thrown after bad. Eventually the crunch will come and it is better to be prevented by a 'difficult' bank manager from going too far down the slippery slope. It is clearly better to cut your losses as soon as it is realised that you are in a 'no-win' situation and get out before things get worse.

Some ways and means to get a better deal from your bank and at least keep down the cost of any loans are described in Appendix 1.

The key factor

It can always be argued that a business which failed as the result of a negative cash-flow was undercapitalised in the first place. This is a common reason put forward by bank managers who have put up the (secured) capital on the basis of a business plan prepared to the bank's own standards and design. In other words, the bank was satisfied with the calculation of the capital required when the loan was agreed but now, with hindsight, is telling you that the business is not soundly based.

There are of course cases where, having raised the necessary capital, the businessman spends it unwisely on such things as expensive cars, luxury office furniture, non-essential equipment and the like. Yielding to this temptation can result in a shortage of cash for the really essential items and to bridge the time gap between spending money and getting some back.

Normally, however, the key factor in the scenario is *getting the money in from debtors*. This is the most sensitive and critical part of the cash-flow cycle and, if other aspects of financial management are reasonably well managed, makes the difference between success and failure.

The fact is that prompt payment can only be expected if an effective strategy is worked out and continuously applied. This strategy is normally even more important than controlling wastage, avoiding idle time, having efficient layouts of factory equipment and all the other factors which have a bearing on ultimate profit.

A company can have the finest product, the lowest possible level of wastage, a superb sales record and the most dedicated work force of all time but if it does not get paid it will die.

It is not enough to mail out the company invoices and then concentrate all one's energies on production, sales or whatever, assuming that the customers will be champing at the bit waiting to pay up.

The strategy to achieve prompt payment should form part of the businessman's overall control of his working capital and will be most effective if part of a complete operating plan. The essential financial aspects of this plan are described in the next chapter.

The cash-flow scene: Key Points

1. Be aware of the cash-flow merry-go-round and its dangers.
   e.g. Make sure, if you are starting a business, that you are adequately funded and avoid unnecessary expenditure on such items as expensive cars or office furniture.

2. A *strategy* for getting money from customers is essential. It will not happen just by itself.

══ 2 ══

WELL MANAGED WORKING CAPITAL

- What is working capital?
- The working capital merry-go-round
- The lead-time calculation
- A golden rule
- Is bigger more beautiful?
- Using a cash-flow forecast
- Smoothing out your payments
- Well-managed working capital: Key Points

What is working capital?

Working capital is anything which does not fall into the category of fixed assets such as machinery, vehicles and buildings.

Generally, working capital is capital which is necessary to cover the cost of goods and services provided to customers and which is used before customers can be charged. There are three categories of working capital:

- **Cash**
  Normally this means the amount of money available from the company bank account.

- **Stocks**
  Stocks include finished goods, raw materials or items bought in for resale.

- **Debtors**
  The money owed to the company by its customers.

It is important to recognise the distinction between the three forms of working capital because they *must* be balanced. In other words the amount held in cash must be sufficient to pay the wages, satisfy the tax man, etc., but the business must also have enough stocks of one kind or another to meet orders received.

At the same time, the only way to convert stocks into cash is by selling them *and receiving the money*. Thus, the amount of working capital tied up in the form of debtors is crucial.

The balancing act is not easy and only too often neglected. This can arise because of an unawareness that both stocks and debtors form part of the working capital and both are allowed to grow too large while the businessman is concerning himself only with the cash.

It must also be recognised that the *true* working capital available is not just the total of cash, stocks and debtors. From these must be subtracted the amount owed to creditors.

This sounds obvious but 'George' was typical of a businessman who overlooked the point. Not long before being forced to wind up his business he proudly stated that he had over £15,000 in the bank. He was also owed quite a lot of money. However he overlooked the fact that he owed:

- £11,000 to suppliers of materials
- £350 accumulated gas and electricity bills
- two-thirds of a quarterly rent of £3000
- VAT of about £1000

George had very little in the way of raw material stocks and, when a major customer delayed payment, George found himself unable to pay his bills *and* pay his employees' wages *and* finance new business. George sadly wound up his business. He had fallen into the trap of confusing liquidity with profit.

The working capital merry-go-round

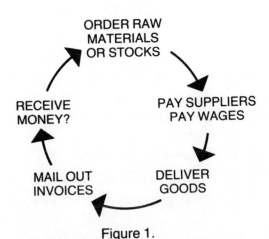

Figure 1.
**The working capital merry-go-round.
(Note the question mark)**

The 'working capital process' is commonly illustrated by a cycle of events as shown in Figure 1.

This way of illustrating the series of events is however

misleading. In real life things are more complicated – and tougher.

Businesses do not, for example, pay their employees once and only after money is received by the business. They are being paid all the time, even if no goods or services are being supplied to customers. Nor are materials necessarily purchased in nice neat packages in response to an order received. This may indeed be a very uneconomic method of purchasing.

Most important, however, is that such interpretations leave out the vital factor of timing.

The chances are that before money is received from the customer it will be necessary to fork out more money on another lot of raw materials to satisfy another order. This may have to be paid for long before the payment is received in respect to the first order.

Clearly for some businesses such as retail stores the problem is reduced if all sales are on a cash basis, but even then there can be a problem if the goods are still on the shelf and unsold when the supplier's bill comes in.

The lead-time calculation

An essential requirement in keeping control of the merry-go-round is knowing the likely time which will elapse between spending money and getting it back. For example:

Time taken to produce the goods	40 days
Time finished goods are in store before delivery	5 days
Time before customer pays	70 days
TOTAL:	115 days

This calculation (based of course on averages and 'best estimates') indicate that wages and other running costs must be met for 115 days before any money can be expected to come in. If, in addition, suppliers have to be paid within, say, 45 days, then they will have to be satisfied $115 - 45 = 70$ days before the customer pays up.

Such calculations help to determine how much cash the company will need to finance its operations and, although unlikely to be wholly accurate, are better than 'flying blind'.

In addition, having worked out the lead-time, the cost of the time that it takes for customers to pay is more easily seen. This is a factor very frequently overlooked in the small business. If, for example, the business is paying 2% above base rate to borrow money, then that is the cost of the outstanding customer debt. In effect, the business is borrowing at a price and lending the money, or some of it, to a customer for nothing.

A further refinement of the lead-time calculation is to add in the average time that raw materials are held in stock before being used. Any excessive time suggests that stocks are out of balance with the other forms of working capital.

A golden rule

These calculations all lead to meeting a 'golden rule' of any business – 'keep working capital to a minimum'. The reason for this rule is simple enough. Capital locked up in stocks or outstanding debts is money which has been neutralised. It cannot be used to finance operations which will expand the business and produce more profit. You may, of course, have good reason for not wishing to expand.

Is bigger more beautiful?

Attempts at expansion can spell the end of a hitherto profitable business. The reason once again is the financing of the operation and the even greater effect that debtors can have.

Expansion normally means taking on larger premises, more staff, more vehicles and equipment and so on. This means a fairly sudden increase in costs which, for the time being and until sales expand *and the money comes in*, puts greater pressure on

11

the business. If the lead-time to get money in stays the same then disaster can be the result. A valuable concept – breakeven point – which should be taken into account when considering expansion is described in Appendix 2.

Much the same problem can arise in the simpler case of taking on a new, large customer who places big orders.

> A real-life case occurred with a small, specialist building company. A new customer came along and gave the company a couple of fairly large orders. Only one of these had been paid for when the new customer offered a very large contract which was accepted with delight and enthusiasm.
>
> The owner of the company felt that he was now in the big time. The crunch came when, having worked on the contract for three months (with no payment received from the previous one), he ran out of money. When asked why he went on so long as to go broke the owner replied:
>
> 'Once I started I couldn't stop. I was unable to go back and I did not want to damage my relationship with *a good customer*.'

A customer who does not pay is not a *good* customer and if the owner had thought about the lead-time and his resources he might have done the right thing by refusing the contract. Alternatively he might have accepted it having negotiated some money up-front plus settlement of the already overdue account.

Using a cash-flow forecast

Such traps and impending problems can be avoided by using a cash-flow forecast. The forecasts (which need regular revision) should form a key part of the financial control process. They enable the business to spot danger periods in the future and also highlight the effects of outstanding debts.

Details of how to prepare a cash-flow forecast are readily available from a variety of sources – including banks. Most banks will provide self-explanatory forms on which forecasts can be constructed. Essentially the forecast is a statement, month by month, of payments the business must make and receipts it expects to enjoy.

By subtracting each month's expected payments from that month's expected income a balance will be obtained which is carried forward to the next month. Realistic assessments of *when* money will be received by the business are as essential as those for *how much* will be received. The effect of any success in speeding up receipts can then be quickly assessed. Sometimes the forecast will indicate that if there is not some speeding up the business will be insolvent at some point in the future. This at least enables the owners to look for more capital before disaster strikes or to step up the pressure to get money in from customers.

These then are some of the essential aspects of managing the working capital which form an essential background to the question of debt collecting. In summary, the basic requirements are:

1. To keep the right balance between the three types of working capital: cash, stock, debts.

2. To ensure that the *true* level of working capital is known by keeping track of amounts owed to creditors. This must include accrued costs such as rent and electricity supplies, for which a bill has not yet been received.

3. To recognise the time element in cash-flow and to take account of lead-times.

4. To keep working capital to a minimum, e.g. by avoiding unnecessarily high stocks of raw materials or finished product. This amounts to 'neutralised' money.

5. To distinguish between liquidity and profit.

6. To be able to recognise and avoid taking on too much, e.g. by using a regularly updated cash-flow forecast and keeping an eye on the breakeven point.

Smoothing out your payments

Reference has already been made to the need to pay *your* suppliers and hopefully the best possible credit terms have been negotiated to avoid, as far as possible, the credit time you get being less than the credit time you give.

There is, in addition, another way to keep your working capital in balance. This is to avoid committing the business to paying out large amounts of money to acquire facilities which can be 'rented'.

An example of this is the so-called 'Facilities Management' offered by computer companies. Your business may have grown to the point where you feel that you need a mainframe computer, albeit a small one. You can probably rent or lease the computer you need – which is a way of avoiding a single massive payout.

However you may not be able to do this and, even if you do, you will have other unavoidable costs.

These can include:

● Building and equipping a computer room.

● Buying in stocks of disks, special cabinets, listing paper, etc.

You will also need to pay a computer operator and possibly a systems analyst and a programmer or two.

All of this, including recruitment costs, can represent a sizeable slice of expenditure which, if translated into net profit terms, will represent a substantial volume of sales. Delays in obtaining the money from these sales will be even more painful as a result of your expenditure on the new facilities.

The Facilities Management (or contract agency service) option enables you to obtain your computer services by means of a monthly fee. The contracting company takes on the job of producing the reports etc. that you need, on their computer and using their staff. This smooths out your payments and relieves you of the management burden. You will also be relieved of the need to take on specialist staff – who are costly and may at times not be fully employed.

This option can possibly be exercised in areas other than computing, for example:

- product testing

- sales campaigns, e.g. mail shots

- research and development

- specialised engineering processes

- transport.

Apart from avoiding the capital expenditure it is likely that the contracted-out services will work out cheaper as a result of economies of scale in the agency operation and the application of skills which the agency company should have.

You will have the added advantage of using the agency services only when you need them and avoid paying for your own costly equipment and people when they are not fully utilised.

Well-managed working capital: Key Points

1. Be aware of what constitutes your working capital.

2. Keep the different types of working capital – cash, stock, debts – in balance.

3. Be aware of the working capital merry-go-round and its complications.

4. Calculate payment lead-times and allow for them when planning your business operations.

5. Stick to the golden rule – 'Keep working capital to a minimum'.

6. Be sure that you want to expand – or to take on larger than usual contracts. If so, work out the cash-flow implications.

7. Do use a cash-flow forecast – continually.

8. Find ways to avoid large, one-off, slugs of expenditure by means of Facilities Management or other agency services.

3

THE DEBTOR PROBLEM – FIRST STAGE PREVENTION

- Some dirty tricks
- How can you circumvent delays?
- Trading overseas
- Taking some insurance
- The ECGD scheme
- First stage prevention: Key Points

17

EVEN if delays in being paid never actually reach the point of bankrupting your business, they are still damaging it.

They are at least restricting your freedom to develop your business by keeping out of your hands the money you may need for new machinery or other desirable changes.

It is not impossible that your customer is actually using your money to develop *his* business. The money he owes you amounts to an interest-free loan, and as long as you give it to him he will use it.

Some dirty tricks

It has been alleged in the business press that some of the large supermarket chains have been able to expand their businesses by this method. By obtaining credit from their suppliers on the one hand and selling those same supplies for cash over the counter on the other they have had an interest-free fund with which to open new branches and finance take-overs.

Many of the suppliers will be small businesses anxious to obtain contracts from the big boys. The result is that small businesses are borrowing from the banks at ruinous rates of interest for the benefit of large companies who are exploiting their power in the market.

The lengths to which unscrupulous financial controllers will go to in the larger companies are horrifying.

One company is, at the time of writing, rewarding its employees with bonuses if they can find ways to delay payment of bills.

An example of the dirty tricks department at work comes from an internationally-known company which, some years ago, was in the process of financing an expansion. This is what I was told by an employee of the company at the time:

'Instructions had gone out to delay all payments as long as possible – except to major suppliers whose goodwill must not be damaged. The smaller suppliers, especially those working in a highly competitive market, were to be stalled.

A small supplier was particularly persistent in chasing for his money and eventually he turned up in person asking for payment. Knowing that he was coming, the accountant had a cheque written out ready for him complete with the accountant's signature. When the supplier arrived he was shown the cheque and told that, as he could see, payment was about to be made. However, he was informed, the cheque required two signatures and the other signatory was temporarily out of the office. The accountant assured the supplier that as soon as the second signature had been obtained the cheque would be his. There was no need to wait, he was told, as the cheque would be in the post that night. Satisfied, the supplier went away. As soon as he left the office the accountant tore up the cheque.'

The small supplier went broke and the bill, I was told, was never paid.

The experiences of a solicitor in pursuing debts on behalf of his clients reveal other little strategies used by the unwilling payer.

The solicitor would normally only become involved when the debt was long overdue, say 4–6 months, and his client had given up hope of obtaining payment by persuasion. The solicitor's first action would usually be a firm but polite letter setting out the facts and demanding payment without further delay. This letter would be ignored and a second one would be sent after two or three weeks threatening legal action if payment was not received within 14 days.

A cheque would arrive on the thirteenth or fourteenth day for the amount outstanding. However, this cheque would have no signature – or, in the case of the more cunning debtor, would have only one signature where two are required.

The missing signature may not be noticed and the cheque would be presented to the bank. In due course the bank would return the cheque and another letter to the debtor would be required.

After a few more days the debtor would reply offering profuse apologies and enclosing a new cheque.

In the more extreme cases this cheque, although properly signed, would include a discrepancy between the written amount and the figures. This would result in either the solicitor having to point out the discrepancy or once again, if the discrepancy had not been spotted, the bank returning the cheque. This process of 'regrettable errors' could gain two or three more weeks of delay for the debtor and ever-increasing solicitor's charges for the creditor.

Other variations on the theme include cheques with no date, cheques written in January with the previous year's date, or unsigned alterations to words or figures.

The motive behind this type of behaviour is considerable. A major company could at any one time owe, say, 100 suppliers an average of £5000 each. As long as these debts are unpaid the company will have an interest-free loan of half a million pounds to do what it likes with.

The profits of the larger insurance brokers are substantially enhanced by the investment earnings on the premiums they have collected from their clients but not passed on to the underwriting insurers.

With premium flows amounting to millions of pounds a year a substantial gain can be made – at the expense of the company to whom the money belongs.

Let us summarise some of the reasons why bills are paid late – or not paid at all:

- The debtor is short of cash – quite possibly because *his* debtors are slow in paying.

- Your invoice contained an error, was sent to the wrong address or offered some other reason for the customer to delay payment. (This particular problem is examined in Chapter Four.)

- The debtor has made a genuine mistake, e.g. he has lost or misfiled your invoice or simply overlooked it.

- The debtor is deliberately delaying payment in order to obtain the benefit of 'free financing'.

- The debtor's payment system is a rigid and bureaucratic one involving one or more of the following:
  - elaborate approval procedures
  - time-consuming matching of invoices to order numbers and job records
  - routine computer runs, without which payments cannot be made
  - a company rule that payments are made on statements, not on individual invoices.

- The debtor is going out of business or has already ceased trading.

How can you circumvent delays?

Prevention of losses and the cost of borrowing money as a result of overdue payments is better than cure, so what can be done by the small and hungry business?

All or some of the following are worth trying:

1. Look before you leap

Asking for and taking up references is an action too often neglected by small businesses. Eagerness to accept an order or a fear that asking for references will offend the customer are common causes of this precaution being neglected.

However, experience shows that in reality the chance of losing the order is small. The probability is that the customer himself asks for references when appropriate and in many cases the customer's respect for the supplier will be increased. Of course, a satisfactory reference does not guarantee fast payment, but (a) it puts the customer on notice that you are professional and will not be treated lightly; and (b) it reduces the chance that you will suffer as a result of doing business with a company lacking the funds to pay its way.

The first requirement in taking up references is a letter to your would-be customer. It could be along the following lines:

21

Thank you for your order no. 1234 for 1000 cast iron widgets and 500 plated widgets.

We will be pleased to supply these products, but as we have not done business with you before we would be grateful for the names of referees.

Please let us have the name and address of your bankers and your account number, and details of two trade referees. Following satisfactory replies from the referees we will fill your order without delay.

We do hope that you will understand the reasons for this precaution and look forward to a mutually beneficial relationship with you in the future.

Having received the details requested, a suitable letter must be sent to the referees. The purpose is to obtain specific information, not a vaguely worded and general response. Your letter must therefore ask specific questions; it could be worded as follows:

Messrs Bloggs and Jones have given us your name as a referee. We would be grateful for the following information:

1. How long you have been doing business with Bloggs and Jones, and in what capacity – e.g. suppliers, consultants, partners?

2. Whether or not Bloggs and Jones have met their obligations to you in a satisfactory manner, in particular whether or not their payments to you have been made on time.

3. The level of credit you are prepared to grant them.

4. Whether or not you would recommend them as customers.

We enclose a stamped, addressed envelope for your reply, but if you prefer to telephone please ask for Mrs Brown on extension 100.

Your help will be much appreciated.

The small courtesy of enclosing an SAE encourages a reply and helps to show that you appreciate the work you are asking the referee to take on.

Note also that the option of a telephoned reply is given. This may be more convenient for the referee and, where there is some doubt about the customer, a more 'comfortable' way of dealing with the enquiry. Some referees are reluctant to make unfavourable comments in writing, for fear of a libel action, but most people in this position are willing to issue a verbal warning, or at least drop a hint, over the telephone.

Should you receive any unclear, incomplete or ambiguous replies to your initial letter, you may find a follow-up telephone call worth while for the same reason. There may be an underlying fear of libel, and the telephone call may help to bring out more facts.

A bank will normally respond to your enquiry by sending you a fairly standard reply in the form of a 'Status Report' indicating the financial standing of the potential customer, i.e. that he is good for £X000. This report will also confirm that he is who he says he is: claims that a company is, say, a trader in commodities, agricultural engineers or whatever are not always true. Letter-headings, and claims made on them, are not wholly reliable. The length of time that the company has been trading and how long they have held an account with the bank will also be indicated in the report.

If you prefer, your own bank will provide a status report service, for a fee, making enquiries with the customer's bank and advising you of the result. This method can be particularly helpful, as your bank will have a vested interest in ensuring that you do not run into trouble. They can, in all probability, dig out more specific information, and will at least give you a broad hint if they have doubts.

If, for any reason, asking for references is not an option then, at least, enquiries can be made among business friends and acquaintances who might be expected to be able to provide some guidance. A reputation for slow payment spreads fast and spreads wide and a few telephone calls can save you a lot of worry and expense in future.

More will be said on the subject of finding out about a potential customer in Chapter Four.

2. Ask for money up-front

This is another measure much neglected for fear that it may offend the customer. Once again it is an exaggerated fear. The order *might* be lost as a result of asking for a part payment in advance but if it is lost it is indicative of a customer who would probably turn out to be a slow payer (or even a non-payer).

> A small business offering a consultancy service, having suffered a bad debts problem, adopted the policy of asking for an advance of fees in every case. The partners in the business reached this conclusion reluctantly and after much heart-searching. Two years later the senior partner doubted if they had lost any business at all for this reason but was certain of one thing – the firm's cash-flow position had improved immensely. The improvement in their financial position has been sufficient to finance an expansion of the business and to place them higher up the league in terms of both market share *and reputation*.

When payment in full is required before the goods will be despatched, the *proforma invoice* is used.

This is a means of obtaining *all* the money up-front, and is sometimes used as an alternative to asking for referees in the case of a new and unknown customer. When two or three transactions have been satisfactorily completed on proforma terms, and confidence has been built up, credit terms may be granted.

Here we have, in effect, a cash-with-order system such as is commonly used in mail order business. Selling by mail order is often attractive simply because payment in advance is an accepted practice. However, cash-with-order must not be used simply as a way to finance purchase or manufacture. The law requires that the goods be ready for sale at the time that the offer to sell (e.g. by advertisement) is made.

3. Specifically negotiate the terms of payment

In many cases the goods or services are supplied before any negotiation on payment terms takes place. The supplying company usually sends out its invoice with the words 'Payment in 30 days' (or similar) typed on the bottom. This hopeful statement will probably not even be noticed by the customer and, if it is noticed, will probably be ignored.

Much the same treatment is received when elaborate contracts are signed. The clause dealing with payment terms will simply be ignored.

In cases such as unusually large orders, or where a new customer is involved, it is far better specifically to discuss the payment terms in advance, negotiate an agreed period and confirm the arrangement by letter. One advantage of this approach is that the negotiation must have taken place with a particular individual – not normally in the customer's accounts department – to whom complaint can be made if a delay occurs. Frequently the individual concerned will, when you contact him, be irritated or embarrassed by the delay and will put pressure on his accounts department to speed things up. Naturally the higher up the management hierarchy that you negotiate the terms, the greater the chance that they will be adhered to.

Among the terms which may be specifically negotiated are:

- a percentage up-front

- payments on completion of clearly definable stages, e.g. on building contracts, completing of footings, walls, roof, etc. can trigger a pre-arranged payment

- credit given for returned containers, faulty parts, etc.

- payments for after-sales service waived or reduced

- fees for training, e.g. given to the customer's employees in the use of machines or handling toxic substances, waived or reduced

- cancellation of payments for spare parts (having agreed that they may be returned if not used)

- instruction manuals or drawings provided free of charge

- delivery charges waived

- insurance costs, e.g. in the case of leased goods, borne by the supplier

'Variables' such as these can be offered to ensure a reduced period/amount of debt.

4. Unity is strength

There are many trade associations in existence such as the Equipment Leasing Association, the Institute of Arbitrators, the British Exhibition Contractors Association and so on.

Some trade associations provide support to their members in cases of dispute by means of legal aid, advice and various forms of pressure. Membership of such a body should be mentioned on company letter heads, contracts and invoices to show that if there is a problem your company is not alone.

A first-class example of what a trade association can do was illustrated in 1989. The Society of Authors, which represents many hundreds of writers, having carried out a survey amongst its members, published a report on their experiences with publishers. Among the various topics examined, promptness of payment of royalties loomed large. Authors, rightly or wrongly, have complained long and hard about delays in payment from certain publishers. The worst offenders were revealed by the report. The Society of Authors could, as a result of the publicity, reasonably expect an improvement in performance for the following reasons:

- Authors, working alone and without the assistance of an agent, would in appropriate cases have their fears that their treatment was unreasonable confirmed. As a result, these authors could choose to seek other publishers (i.e. those who showed up well on the report), thus removing from the poor payers their source of 'raw material'.

- Authors' agents would be pressed by their clients to offer new work to the better payers.

- Publishers with a bad record would be prompted to consider carefully their future performance in their dealings with authors.

As a direct result of this sort of action the Society of Authors has also obtained for its members much improved contractual terms with a number of publishers.

In addition to the potential value of membership of trade associations small businesses can help themselves – if indirectly – by supporting organisations which will work for them. Examples in the UK are the Small Business Research Trust, the Forum of Private Business and the National Federation of Self-employed and Small Businesses.

Such organisations lobby political parties and governments to obtain a better deal for small businesses including, in recent years, pressure for legislation to protect the small business from slow payers. These organisations also draw attention to the other side of the coin – the high interest rates which small businesses endure in order to finance their businesses and the cash gap caused by slow payment. Pressure is applied to government in particular to introduce schemes – such as exist in some continental European countries – to provide low-cost finance.

In West Germany, for instance, the Reconstruction Credit Bank provides more than four billion pounds a year in cheap finance for small businesses.

5. Retaining the title

The Sale of Goods Act 1979 provides that title to goods passes from seller to buyer when the terms of the contract specify. In other words, if the contract is appropriately worded title to the goods need not pass at the time of sale or delivery. A clause can be written into a contract stipulating that until the goods are paid for they remain the property of the supplier. This, one would think, would be of considerable value in hastening payment and in the prevention of bad debts. It is not, however, quite as simple as it sounds: in fact it is one of those cases where the lawyers can get rich and everyone else very frustrated.

Much depends on the circumstances. If, for example, the goods supplied are perishable (e.g. fruit and vegetables) or otherwise deteriorate with the passage of time (e.g. paint, certain pharmaceuticals and cement) then they will probably not be worth repossessing once it is clear that payment has become a problem.

Similarly, if the goods are 'merged' with something else they may not be 're-possessable' at all. This would be the case if, say, paint and wallpaper were supplied and they were used to redecorate an office building.

However, with many manufactured goods title retention does offer some protection against non-payment providing the supplier can readily identify his goods by means of serial numbers, batch numbers or similar identifying marks and codes.

Should your customer become insolvent, the goods for which you have retained title (and can positively identify) will be beyond the reach of the receiver and any other anxious creditors.

In the event that your widgets – for which you have retained title – have been incorporated into something made by your customer and sold on to a third party you *may* still have some protection. Whether or not you would succeed in such a case will depend on whether or not you can establish a prior right (over the receiver) for that portion of the proceeds of sale which relates to your widgets. Since a famous case (the Romalpa case) of 1976, rights to the proceeds of sale have been attacked on the grounds that the ultimate purchaser did not hold the goods in trust for the original supplier, i.e. there was no fiduciary relationship between them.

You will see that there are, to say the least, complications and limitations in using a retention clause in your contracts. There is nevertheless value in such a clause. It is likely that the threat of repossession will carry weight with a customer even when he is on the verge of insolvency. Repossession could result in his inability to carry on business at all, and you may well gain priority over other creditors who cannot apply the same amount of muscle.

The wording of your contract and any title retention is best done with the advice of a solicitor who specialises in the field of trading terms and sales contracts. A good lawyer should know how to get the best protection despite the potential complications.

Trading overseas

Weigh up the export market

Many small to medium businesses are reluctant to trade overseas due to fears (often unjustified) of the paperwork problems, uncertainty about procedures and the problem of being paid.

The latter fear is only too understandable when reports appear in the press describing how much money major banks have to set aside as loan-loss provision in respect to foreign clients. In 1989, Midland Bank set aside £1.36 billion against an exposure of £4.27 billion. Lloyds, with a debt exposure of £3.79 billion has set aside 34% of this amount. Other banks, both in the UK and in other European countries, have similar problems. If the major banks end up out of pocket as a result of *loans* to *governments*, it might fairly be asked what chance the small business has in selling to overseas customers.

The answer, perhaps, is to look at the type of clients to whom the banks have chosen to lend money and then avoid those geographical areas like the plague. It is not necessary to be an expert on foreign political systems to know where the major risks are to be found.

The countries to be avoided are those which exhibit some or all of the following features:

- A high cost of living normally associated with a startling rate of inflation. In such territories there could well be an overvalued exchange rate which could collapse at any time.

- Social instability. Oppressive policing, demonstrations and riots combined with a history of coups d'état are danger signs. The chances are that your customer may become politically unacceptable in the case of yet another military takeover and could disappear from the scene.

- Corruption. In some countries corruption is commonplace with a percentage for the politicians, customs officials or whoever else can obtain a rake-off. All of this means that the normal rules of business do not apply and unscrupulous customers can take the shirt off your back.

- Foreign exchange restrictions There are countries in which importers must obtain government approval to use foreign currencies or to send money abroad – or both. Obtaining such approvals can take as much as two or even three years, however much your customer is willing to pay you.

Common sense should apply when considering an export order and, if there is any doubt, advice can be obtained. UK companies can, for example, ask for advice from the Department of Trade.

These warnings should be regarded as such and not as an all-embracing argument against export business. Such business, properly conducted, can be very rewarding.

Export contracts

Another important action neeeded to minimise loss in exporting is to ensure that your contract with the buyer is a sound one. It is not uncommon for exporters to enter into forms of contract which reduce or remove their rights of redress against the buyer if anything should go wrong. Clauses relating to retention of title to the goods can be vital, and it is no bad thing to have provision whereby the buyer pays default interest. Some good legal advice is worth paying for to ensure that your contracts for export business are sound.

The practicalities of business mean that from time to time it may be unavoidable or even desirable to depart from your normal terms of trade. This is especially the case in export trading where deliveries can be delayed by strikes or bad weather at sea – or any number of causes. There can also be temporary problems which your customer may face, often caused by circumstances beyond his control.

You may, in such cases, judge that it is in your interests to permit some variation from the contract or to make some other concession to your customer. It is important in such circumstances not to allow the variation or concession to be regarded as a permanent change to your contractual relationship with your customer or a precedent to changed trading conditions.

To safeguard your future position a declaration should be made *in writing* making your position clear. The concession to which you have agreed should be clearly and precisely described and then followed by a statement such as this:

> . . . the above arrangement has been entered into without creating a precedent for the future and should on no account be deemed to be construed as a waiver of our contractual rights, limits or defences under our standard trading conditions.

Protection from a Bill of Lading

When goods are exported by sea the contract of carriage between the seller of the goods and the carrier (the shipowner or ship charterer) is represented by a Bill of Lading.

The Bill of Lading is handed to the seller by the carrier with the clear understanding that the goods, having arrived in the port of destination, will not be handed over to anyone except on presentation of the Bill of Lading. This means that the buyer must be given the Bill of Lading by the seller.

This arrangement provides a means for the seller to ensure that he will be paid. The way that this is done is as follows:

1. The seller provides the buyer with the name and address of his bank and the name of a correspondent bank in the buyer's country.

2. The buyer arranges for sufficient funds to be deposited in the correspondent bank to cover the value of the goods being shipped.

3. The seller deposits the Bill of Lading with his bank.

4. When the correspondent bank confirms that the necessary funds have been received the seller's bank sends them the Bill of Lading. The funds are then transferred to the seller's bank.

5. The buyer is given the Bill of Lading by the correspondent bank when confirmation of the transfer of funds is received and he can now use it to collect the goods.

This system (rather similar to a cash-on-delivery arrangement) offers substantial protection to the buyer. The Bill of Lading is a standard form of shipping contract which has been used for many centuries. There are, unfortunately, many cases of fraud in which forged Bills of Lading are presented to the carrier who then hands over the goods to a person not entitled to them. Should this happen, the seller can sometimes successfully sue the carrier or his agent in the port of destination for the value of the goods. Care should be taken to ensure that the contract of carriage places full responsibility on the carrier and that both he and his agent are fully insured.

Taking some insurance

It is possible within limits to buy insurance cover against losses as a result of a customer's inability to pay you.

There is a limited insurance 'market' in the United Kingdom for this cover with a special scheme for exporters run by the Export Credit Guarantee Department (ECGD).

The ECGD scheme is generally wider in its scope and nature

than those provided by private insurers and will be explained later.

The private market offers insurance of trade credit against non-payment by a customer through *insolvency*. In other words, your customer must have gone bust before the insurance cover comes into play.

However, the insurers may also offer support in the form of information about companies – both home and abroad – which you may be considering as customers. One insurance company claims to have details of more than a million companies in the UK alone. This information can be of considerable assistance in evaluating business opportunities and can provide an early warning of unusual risk. Naturally, the insurers will not themselves wish to offer insurance cover in cases where the chance of having to pay up on a claim is high. Their views on the business you are contemplating can be worth listening to.

Cover can normally be obtained on an across-the-board basis in which all your trading is insured or, if preferred, cover can be restricted to a part of your business or even to one particularly large contract. Insuring one large contract can be an especially valuable facility for the expanding small business. It is often the case that the 'breakthrough' into a newer and higher level of turnover can depend on and result from a single major contract of much greater size than those normally undertaken. There will in all probability be a requirement to spend unusually large sums of money on materials and labour which can stretch the working capital of the business. A bank loan or other form of additional finance may have been obtained, and should the customer go to the wall before he has paid for the goods or services the result could be catastrophic.

Selecting the business you wish to insure and taking all the risk yourself in cases where you judge this risk to be low can make economic sense. The premiums for credit insurance are expensive and should only be paid when the risk to you is high. Measurement of the risk to *you* may be different from the measurement of the risk to the insurer. It could be that the loss of, say, £10,000 would be a disaster for your business but would not be a problem for a well-established insurance company.

It is important to distinguish between the probability of loss and the damage that the loss will cause. For example you may be quite willing to take a chance on a £100 contract even if the probability of loss is fairly high. Such a sum of money is unlikely to form a significant part of your cash flow. On the other hand a £10,000 loss *will* have a significant effect and, even if the probability of disaster striking is relatively low, taking some insurance may be a very prudent step. Creating your own reserves against a bad debt can restrict your activities – even if you have the liquidity available.

The advice of a competent insurance broker with specialist knowledge in the field of credit insurance should be sought.

The scope of cover, costs and back-up services can vary from one insurer to another and some professional help can prevent problems.

The ECGD scheme

The main service provided by the Export Credit Guarantee Department is insurance against the risk of non-payment by overseas customers.

Cover is not limited to non-payment as a result of insolvency. The action of foreign governments in preventing payments by, say, the imposition of exchange controls, is a familiar cause of trouble and this can be covered.

The ECGD also provide cover for the buyer's failure to pay within six months after the due date for goods accepted and also the buyer's failure or refusal to accept goods despatched which comply with the contract.

In addition, they offer protection against war and civil war, outside the UK, preventing performance of the contract – even where the cause of loss is not normally commercially insurable.

Security such as this can be vitally important, especially where trading with countries which are liable to sudden political upheaval. However, the security is desirable even when there has been no history or warning of trouble. Few exporters to

Argentina would have been able to forecast the Falklands war!

The ECGD offers a Short Term Guarantee for exports sold on terms of payment up to 180 days. The guarantee scheme involves a system of credit control based on 'credit limits' worked out for individual buyers. These credit limits stipulate, for each overseas buyer, the maximum amount that you may have outstanding at any one time for goods despatched. The credit limits are established in two ways. Firstly, the Short Term Guarantee will indicate two discretionary limits which, at the time of writing, are one of £5000 and one of £20,000. These limits enable you to trade up to £5000 with a new customer and to progressively raise the volume to £20,000 outstanding on a buyer with whom you have traded satisfactorily in the past.

If you wish to exceed your discretionary limits this must be agreed with ECGD which will make its own judgement of the size of the credit limit that can be agreed.

Some businessmen may see these limits as an irritating restriction on their freedom to trade. This is a mistaken attitude. The fact is that a small to medium business is most unlikely to have all the information needed to accurately assess the risk involved in export trading. ECGD, who have a substantial database covering many thousands of buyers, will be in a much better position to make a sensible judgement. This is a positive protection for the supplying company who should regard the credit limits allowed as a shield against disaster.

The credit limit, once agreed, is normally valid for two years, but can be varied or cancelled in the meantime as a result of a change in your customer's circumstances. You are not limited to working strictly within the agreed credit limits – you can, for example, enter into a contract of much greater value providing that shipments are spread out over a period of time.

If properly organised, the amount outstanding at any one time will remain within the credit limit.

The ECGD are well aware of the urgency with which deals must be concluded at times. They claim to deal with credit limit applications within 24 hours in 70% of cases.

Full details of the ECGD scheme are available from their head office:

ECGD Insurance Services
Crown Building, Cathays Park, Cardiff CF1 3NH Tel: (0222) 824000 Telex: 497305 Fax: (0222) 824003

There are also branch offices in nine other major cities whose addresses can be found in the local telephone directory. The ECGD provide a number of well written booklets describing their services.

A valuable additional opportunity

Once you have ECGD cover for your export business, a number of organisations will be prepared to provide you with finance. One of the major UK banks, for instance, offers 100% finance of export invoices – subject to a maximum annual export turnover of £100,000. Such credit is available for a maximum of 180 days and the bank's interest in the transaction is not disclosed to your customer. As far as he is concerned he is dealing with you alone.

These, then, are some of the broad, first-stage steps which can be taken to avoid trouble in the first place. In the next chapter we will examine some practical steps which you can take within your own business to reduce the chance that the order you have accepted will not, ultimately, be regretted.

First stage prevention: Key Points

1. Be aware of the 'dirty tricks' which may be played on you.
2. Look before you leap – take up references and make enquiries in the market.
3. Don't be afraid to ask for money up-front.
4. Negotiate the terms of payment – specifically.
5. Join and support any trade associations or other organisations which can support you in improving payment practices or in getting you out of trouble.

6. Keep your eyes wide open when considering export business. Look for the danger signs in the territories concerned.

7. Make sure your export contracts are sound and legally watertight. Guard against concessions which can be used to change contractual relationships to your detriment.

8. Make use of the Bill of Lading method to ensure payment before the goods are handed over.

9. Consider taking out credit insurance – possibly for only the more critical parts of your business. For exporters, the ECGD scheme should be examined.

4

THE DEBT COLLECTING PROCESS – AVOIDING SELF-INFLICTED WOUNDS

- Plan it – to make it happen
- Do you work to an effective system?
- What tends to happen
- A simple system for keeping track
- Know your customer's set-up
- Credit – cash and time limits
- Get it right – first time
- To discount or not to discount?
- Bill small, bill often
- Keeping your ear to the ground
- Are you organised for collecting money?
- A warning to small businesses
- A look into the (near) future
- What is EDI?
- Is EDI for you?
- How to prepare for EDI
- What about the cost?
- Avoiding self-inflicted wounds: Key Points

Plan it – to make it happen

The whole process of getting the money into your bank account starts in *your* office – long before the goods or services are supplied and the invoice despatched. There are a number of small but vital actions which can be taken to reduce the chance of delay in payment and some fundamental procedural requirements to achieve the same result.

Do you work to an effective system?

Many delays in payment start, not in the customer's office but in the supplier's office. Let us see what might happen:

1. An order is received and scheduled into the production programme.

2. The work is done and the customer's needs are met.

3. The fact that the transaction has been completed will be transmitted to the person whose job it is to prepare the sales invoice.

   If a delay of say, five days, takes place before this is done, then a five-day delay in payment has already been created *by the supplying company*. Five days is not an uncommon delay.

   A small printing company (which went bust) was found to allow an average of six working days to elapse before the part-time billing clerk was given the details of a completed job. The owner of the business stated that he could not reduce the delay because he was too busy to work out all the various costs required to produce the invoice.

   In fact this was nonsense – the real cause was that he was not sufficiently disciplined to enter the costs on a job sheet designed for the purpose as and when they arose. At some time *after* the event he would scurry around looking for missing bits of paper on which the various costs were recorded. Since each job was based on a quotation to the customer, most of the scurrying around was in any case unnecessary. The fact was that sometimes the original quote was mislaid and the amount forgotten.

The demise of the company concerned was hastened when the part-time clerk went on holiday for two weeks and no invoices were prepared for three weeks. This resulted in a 'revenue gap' of about a month – during which time costs were accrued and bills had to be paid.

A system is needed to ensure that *as soon as the order is executed* the billing process starts. A copy of a despatch note, or a completed job card, or some other document which indicates what is to be invoiced and to whom, is all that is normally required.

What tends to happen

Let us suppose that the billing clerk has received the signal to prepare an invoice. Further delays can now arise for one or more of the following reasons:

- The order was for Smith & Co. but was it J. Smith & Co. or B. Smith & Co? The production foreman merely scribbled 'Smith' on the job card and now the billing clerk must spend time finding out which customer is involved.

  If, as sometimes happens, the invoice is sent to the wrong customer, then several weeks of delay can result. Even if the recipient immediately recognises that the invoice should have gone to someone else it may be several days before they get round to telling you and sending it back. A further day or two will then go by before the invoice is re-typed and mailed to the correct customer.

- The billing clerk must check each time with the boss as to what is to be charged. How much for delivery? Are we giving a discount and how much? What are we charging for packaging? Are there any disbursements to be included?

41

A busy little company providing a service delayed its invoicing by not having chargeable out-of-pocket expenses totalled and ready for the invoicing procedure. The chargeable man-hours were promptly available from a time-sheet prepared for the job done. But the relevant expenditure on taxi fares, hotel bills and the like – all chargeable to the client – had to be sorted out at the month end when records of expenses were prepared by employees. This meant that a whole month's billing accumulated before any action could be taken, resulting in an average of two weeks' self-inflicted delay.

This delay, it should be noted, was the result of not having a very small part of the total charge available. The fees, which were normally in excess of 90% of the amount to be invoiced, were held up by relatively trivial amounts. The solution was to ask employees to record out-of-pocket expenses on the same form as the man hours, so that as soon as the job was finished the billing clerk could be presented with the full story in one go.

In cases where small amounts such as packaging charges and the like can be made it may be better to work to a standard charge. The billing clerk can then look up the standard charge from a list of charges (which should be regularly revised) and add it to the invoice without more ado.

- No account number has been allocated to a new customer and the clerk puts the papers in a pending tray until the boss gets round to it. Such silly reasons for delay can be removed by delegating the allocation of account numbers, sales area codes and so on to the billing clerk.

  There is rarely any good reason for the boss to be the only person who can make such routine decisions – but it happens.

- Is the billing address the same as the delivery address? Salesmen are often told by the customer that the goods are to be delivered to the customer's factory in, say, Croydon, whilst the invoice should be sent to Head Office in, say, Birmingham. The billing clerk should be informed of this and given the Head Office address. If the salesman leaves out any instructions on the order form, the conscientious clerk will be obliged to take time to check if there is a special invoicing address. A salesman who leaves blank the space for the invoicing address (probably because it is the same as the delivery address) can cause all sorts of trouble. The billing clerk should not have to waste time checking to see if there has been an error of omission.

Another common problem is the omission of the *address* of the place to which the invoice should be sent. The order form will state:

DELIVERY ADDRESS: Unit 9, Trading Estate, Slough, Berks.

INVOICING ADDRESS: Head Office, Birmingham

The billing clerk must now chase around to find out *where* in Birmingham the customer has his office. It is not unknown for salesmen to omit to record *both* delivery address and mailing address!

- Is the invoice for the attention of a particular individual or department?

    This can be an especially important matter. Large customers may well have an extensive office, hundreds of employees and a massive bureaucracy. An invoice addressed simply to the company will follow a process involving:

    – Opening the envelope in the post room.
    – Sending the invoice to the department which the post room supervisor *thinks* is the right one.
    – Finding the right person to approve the payment and, in all probability, allocate a budget code to it.

    All this, which can take several days even if there are no hold-ups, will take place *before* the invoice is sent to the accounts department to be placed in a queue of work for attention. The allocation of inadequately addressed post can take several days in a large office. It is a job which often receives a low priority – particularly if the item is a bill to be paid!

To avoid some of this delay the billing clerk may have to contact the salesman or some other difficult-to-find person to check the name of the addressee. This, in itself, takes time and is a self-imposed delay.

Some of these possible reasons for hold-ups in your invoicing process draw attention to other important preventive measures which can be taken to avoid self-inflicted wounds.

A *simple system for keeping track*

It is important that, having prepared your invoice accurately and without delay, you have a means to keep track of the payment due. Time gained in an efficient preparation process can be lost by a failure to notice that the payment terms are in danger of being exceeded. A system is needed which, if operated in a disciplined way, will keep you aware of the situation.

Such a system need not be complicated and does not depend on the possession and use of a computer.

Manual methods

One simple and cheap method which a small business can use is based on visual control. It works like this:

1. A series of boxes or deep trays are set up labelled 'Current', '30+ days', '60+ days', '90+ days'. The boxes or trays can be of any convenient type suitable for holding standard A4 sheets of paper (or whatever size you use for your invoices and letters). One company used a set of inexpensive vegetable racks purchased from a hardware shop!

2. As soon as an invoice is prepared and mailed to the customer the office copy is placed in the box marked 'Current'.

3. *Each day* the billing clerk examines the invoices in the current box, takes out those which are 30 days old, sends the

appropriate chase-up letter and places the invoice in the '30+ days' box.

4. The contents of the other boxes are likewise examined and appropriate action taken.

This system enables the billing clerk and/or a more senior person responsible for credit control to see at a glance the *general* position. A growing number of invoice copies in the boxes holding the older transactions indicates a worsening situation requiring more action.

The visual control effect can be enhanced by placing a coloured sticker (red is a favourite choice) on each invoice over a chosen value. This enables the person carrying out the daily check to assess not only the number of invoices outstanding but to see how many are of high value.

There are a number of variations which can be applied to this system. One variation is to use ring binders instead of boxes or trays. Another is to keep special binders, boxes or trays for the high value invoices or for selected customers.

Whatever variation is chosen, one thing remains as important and an essential feature of the system. The regular (preferably daily) examination of the invoices must be adhered to. Without this discipline the system will become misleading and potentially costly.

If you have a computer

Readymade computer systems to keep track of unpaid bills are available. Essentially the system works like this:

1. Each sale is recorded on to the computer, via a keyboard, showing customer's name, invoice number, date of invoice and amount due.

2. When payment is received, this is recorded on the computer which automatically marks off the invoice as paid (in full or in part).

3. A list of unpaid items can be viewed on a screen, or printed out, or both.

4. If required, the computer can list all items over, say 30 days since the date of invoicing – or at any other age.

The use of such an aged-debtor listing is further described in Chapter Five.

Know your customer's set-up

Naming names

If you know the *individual* in your customer's organisation who has the power and the responsibility to clear invoices for payment you are immediately in a better position. Not only can invoices be addressed to him to save time, you also have someone to whom you can refer if a payment delay occurs.

Payment schedules

Similarly, it is important to know *how* the customer's payment process works. Many companies are computerised and have a once-a-month purchase ledger run during which cheques are prepared for suppliers. A reasonable guess is that this computer run takes place at month end but that is not always the case.

If you know when the purchase ledger run is carried out you can time your invoicing to fit it. If you are unlucky enough to miss the run by just one day your invoice will sit waiting for action for another month. In the event that your business is so active that you have a pile of invoices to prepare, then knowing the timing used by your customers enables you to put the work in a priority order to gain an advantage.

The billing clerk can give first priority to invoices for customers whose computer run will take place in the next few days rather than missing the run because other, less urgent, invoices are put first. Ideally, of course, *all* invoices will be despatched within 24 hours of completion of the order.

Unhappily, life is not always that simple and some scheduling of the work may be necessary.

Payment on statement

Another useful item of knowledge, which will become self-evident in time, is whether or not the customer pays on invoices or on receipt of a statement. This can be a particular problem in the case of new customers, as a number of invoices can be overdue for payment and chase-ups made before the customer calmly says: 'We always pay on receipt of statements and you have not sent us one.' This rather unfairly throws the ball back into your court and starts another round of delay. You will prepare and mail the required statement, which then has to wait for the month-end computer run, and so the delay goes on. It is important to find out in advance how the customer conducts his affairs so that a statement, even if only covering one item, can be prepared and sent before its absence is used as an excuse for non-payment.

Payment on account

Payment on statement can also provide another delaying tactic for the less scrupulous debtors. This is the old 'payment on account' ploy. The customer owes you, say, £2000 made up of five dissimilar amounts. After some pressure from you to pay up, the customer, who has probably queried *one* of the amounts on the statement, sends you a cheque for, say, £500 'on account'.

This amount will not match any of the items shown on your statement and can be used as a means to hold up further payments whilst you haggle over *which* items can be regarded as paid for and which not.

It is important in such cases never, by carrying forward a total from one month to the next, to lose the individual items from your statements. Once the individual items are 'lost' any amount of confusion can be caused by the customer who can insist that *according to his records* certain items have been paid

47

for – the payment on account being used to cover more than one item and, with luck, counted twice. The use of this ploy is not normally a straight case of an attempt to avoid payment altogether, but by creating confusion can provide an excuse to delay further payment 'until the muddle is sorted out'.

One sole trader goes as far as to avoid ever billing exactly the same amount more than once to a customer during any accounting period. This is to avoid an insistence that the cheque for, say, £100, applied to both of two invoices for that amount. A few pence difference makes each item unique, identifiable and attributable to only one payment.

These are some of the more important things you need to know about your customer. It is not normally difficult to find out how the customer operates by asking him the right questions when the order is being discussed or, subsequently, during day-to-day contact. Knowing what goes on in his offices can save much disappointment, worry and cost.

The effort can be very worth while in cash terms. If for example you have an average of £20,000 outstanding debt and your own profits are, say, 10% then to compensate for the loss of money you must obtain additional orders worth around £200,000.

Another way of looking at it is to say that if the average outstanding debt can be reduced by half and the money put in a safe building society account, this would be worth about 10% of £10,000 per year. A thousand pounds, or whatever, for no effort at all is well worth having. Why give it to your customer?

Checklist of things to find out

Here is a list of questions to ask when visiting a customer, talking to him on the telephone, or on any suitable occasion that crops up:

1. Which individuals can approve payments and what approval limits do they have?

2. Who signs the cheques?

3. Is there a regular payments' run on the computer? If so, when does it take place?

4. If there is no computer in use, is there a regular bill-paying day? If so, when is it?

5. Are payments made on invoices, or only against statements?

6. Is there a different address for invoicing purposes?

7. Is there a buyer who can help you speed up outstanding payments? What is his name and status relative to the manager of the payments department?

A list like this can be given to salesmen, with instructions to complete it as and when they can. The answers should be available to the person who prepares your invoices – preferably in a single binder or other accessible form of storage for customer information.

Credit – cash and time limits

Almost everything is negotiable, including payment terms. It is only too easy to passively accept 'the industry norm' of 70 days, 90 days or whatever period everyone is complaining about. A positive attitude is necessary on the part of the salesman who should confirm that payment terms are, say, 30 days, and bills will be paid within that time. If no attempt is made to confirm the arrangement, the customer will in all probability take advantage of the industry norm – regardless of the terms of payment printed on the back of your invoice. Make your position clear in advance and negotiate a special deal for yourself.

This *is* possible and the small business should not be afraid of laying its cards on the table. You *may* lose a customer once in a while, but probably a bad payer.

This approach need not be limited to new customers. Two young men who run a small business producing tailor-made equipment for a variety of customers have developed a successful policy for negotiating payment terms. At the outset they ask for a 30-day turnaround and, if their customer enjoys a short lead-time (e.g. retailers), some money up-front. They work hard to give the customer exactly what he wants, with an above average service and at reasonable cost. In the event that they have any delay problems they approach the customer and ask for future payments in *less* than thirty days!

Having proved themselves to be reliable suppliers and competitively priced, they have achieved considerable success and at the time of writing enjoy a seven-day (yes, seven-day) turnaround from a regular customer. This customer is a large multi-national which could treat them with some disdain. However, the value of the service is recognised and paid for.

At all times they adopt a friendly approach – an important policy which will be expanded on in a later chapter.

We have not yet, however, dealt with all the basic, mundane but important actions that can be taken to prevent a problem arising.

Get it right – first time

Sufficient effort must go into ensuring that your invoices are accurate and identifiable. Any failure in this respect gives the customer a first-class and justified excuse for delay.

Is the invoice accurate?

Let us suppose we have contracted to supply 200 widgets at £100 each. Due to last-minute production difficulties we were only able to ship 195 widgets. The remaining 5 were despatched later and will be invoiced next week. Unfortunately our billing clerk was not told of this discrepancy and put 200 widgets on the invoice.

A few days later the billing clerk received a job card for 5 more widgets and an invoice was prepared and sent off accordingly.

A month goes by and, having not received a payment for the first consignment of widgets, you telephone the customer. The reply from the customer is likely to be one of the following:

> 'We have never received a delivery of 200 widgets and we cannot reconcile the invoice with a delivery note.'

> 'We agree that you delivered us 195 widgets but we have no trace of an invoice for that amount.'

> 'Your invoice is in my query tray along with another for 5 widgets which we did not order.'

A reply such as this does not necessarily mean that the customer is being deliberately evasive or is stupid. The chances are that the individual responding to the query has hundreds of invoices to deal with each month and is under a lot of pressure. It is natural for such a person to clear the easy work first and, when time allows, sort out the problem cases.

You must make sure that your invoice is one of the easy ones to handle.

Other inaccuracies can include:

- miscalculation of the total price;
- miscalculation of the VAT amount;
- quoting the wrong customer order number.

Mathematical calculations are less a problem when invoices are prepared on a computer *but*, although the machine will work out price extensions, discounts and totals with absolute accuracy, the operator can still feed in the wrong basic data in the first place.

This is only too easy when the billing clerk has to depend on a grubby, grease-stained job sheet on which someone on the production side has scribbled some barely decipherable figures. Fives which look like threes and threes which look like eights can result in an incorrect invoice however much computer power is available. This in turn leads to a dispute and delay.

The customer cannot be relied upon to shorten the delay by querying your incorrect invoice as soon as he sees it. The chances are that he will leave it until he is not so busy and even then will spend time comparing it with his original order and your delivery note. It is by no means uncommon for the error to be revealed and investigation started only after you have started chasing him for payment.

Whatever the case, an error provides a talking point and a reason for delay – apart from the poor image of your company that is being promoted.

Is the invoice identifiable?

All of us must have seen an invoice from time to time which is a complete mystery.

'What the hell is this all about?' is the usual reaction to an invoice which we cannot make head or tail of.

The classic unidentifiable invoice is one which:

- fails to quote the customer's order number or other reference;

- fails to describe the goods, e.g. – 'To Goods £450' instead of 'To supply of 45 Widgets type XYZ';

- fails to indicate individual or departmental information such as:
  - 'For the attention of Mr Snooks'.
  - 'Despatched to Croydon warehouse'.
  - 'Delivered to Research Department on 15 January 1990'.

Such omissions mean that someone in the customer's office has to make enquiries to find out whether or not the invoice is valid, the goods or service actually received and who should approve it.

This type of invoice will also end up on the pile to be attended to 'when I have a moment to spare' and, because it causes additional work, will also irritate the person dealing with it. It does not take many such irritations to create enough dislike of your company among the customer's staff for them to consciously or unconsciously disregard your work in favour of someone else's. Accounts staff are human, too.

To discount or not to discount?

Whether or not it is worth offering a discount for prompt payment is an old argument.

The first consideration is a purely mathematical one: is the cost of the discount at least covered by the financial advantage of having the money earlier? This is a straight case of working out how much the discount costs you (e.g. 1% of invoiced amount), and, *assuming* the time gained, how much this is worth in terms of bank interest or return on investment. Such calculations are of dubious value because of the need to make an assumption about the time gained. It could be that the customer will pay within say, 30 days rather than 60 days in order to enjoy the discount. However, this is not a certainty. He may have paid within 30 days without a discount available to him.

There may be trade practices which make an early payment discount unavoidable, or a company may have found out by trial and error whether the discount is worth it or not.

Perhaps the only fairly certain conclusion that one can come to is that a discount of suitable size (i.e. not too large) is worth offering for immediate payment. In this case we are likely to be comparing immediate money with money received 30 days later – at best.

The other side of the coin, charging interest for overdue amounts, is likely to be unfavourable. In some jurisdictions this practice is illegal without a licence and, in addition to being a first-class way to create a rift with the customer, is anyway very difficult to enforce.

There is no legal right to charge interest on late payments unless this was one of the terms of the contract of sale. The mere provision in the invoice for interest to be paid is not binding on the buyer unless the invoice is a part of the contract of sale.

Whether or not this is the case can be a very tricky legal point, but in general, invoices form good evidence of what was agreed providing they are properly prepared.

Proper preparation requires that all the following information should be provided on the invoice:

- Invoice number and date
- Name and address of buyer
- Complete description of goods sold
- Price including discount (if any)
- Place of delivery
- Time of delivery
- Time of payment and interest charges (if any)
- Purchase order number
- Date of despatch
- Name, address and registered number of selling company
- VAT number of selling company.

Qualified, professional legal advice should be sought before attempting to do business on the basis of charging interest. It is important to ensure that your documentation is sound and will stand up to scrutiny if there is a dispute. You should also be clear as to what constitutes a contract of sale and whether or not some other document is desirable and necessary – in addition to your invoice.

Bill small, bill often

Often a supplier is delivering goods or providing services in a series of small 'packages'. For example, a manufacturer of plastics housewares may despatch 100 buckets on the first of the month, 200 bowls on the fifth, 30 dustbins on the eighth and so on – all to the same customer.

There is a temptation, based on the idea that clerical time and paperwork can be saved, to save up the various transactions and to bill them all under one invoice at the end of the month. Probably time and paperwork *will* be saved but is it worth it?

In the first place, saving up a month's transactions adds an average of two weeks' postponement of receiving payment but also, perhaps even more important, increases the total amount shown on your invoice.

You may well find from experience with your customers that some of them pay smaller debts faster than they pay larger debts. The reasons for this include the following possibilities:

1. The customer's payments clerk is authorised to pay small sums (say, up to £200) on his own authority, but larger sums need the approval of the Chief Accountant or some other senior person.

   Obtaining this approval takes time and if the Chief Accountant is away on business or holiday it can be quite a lengthy time.

   Some companies operate a 'hierarchical' system for approval of payments involving more and more senior people as the amounts increase. If the Chief Accountant and the Managing Director are *both* involved in the approval of your invoice then even more delay can be expected. The chance that both of these busy people are immediately available and willing to sign your cheque is probably remote.

2. Small amounts are subjected to a less rigorous checking process than large amounts. A company dealing with hundreds of purchase invoices each month will probably have found that mathematical checking (e.g. extensions and totals) is not worth the cost in respect to small amounts. Normally the majority of the invoices to be checked represent only a small part of monthly expenditure and it is only the smaller volume of invoices for larger amounts which justify the cost of a check.

   Small invoices are likewise less likely to receive other forms of scrutiny and are often processed in less time.

For these reasons it may be better to add to your paperwork burden for the sake of having smaller invoices which are paid more rapidly.

There is too, another possibility illustrated by a real-life case.

> A company providing goods to a major customer had long adopted the practice of combining two or more deliveries on the same invoice.
>
> Payments were normally made by the customer in reasonable time, but once in a while there was a long delay. In one such situation the manager of the supplying company complained about the delay to his customer. 'Yes,' said the customer's representative. 'There is a delay, but it is due to the way that you prepared the invoice.' He went on to explain that the various items on the invoice were chargeable to different budgets. This meant that the invoice was photocopied a number of times and the copies sent to various people for budget allocation and approvals.
>
> This caused the delay and not a little extra work in the customer's office.

It might reasonably be argued that the customer should have told the supplier about this problem in the first place so that both delay and extra work could be avoided. However, the people who deal with the purchase invoices rarely have any direct contact with the supplier – or they may feel too junior to suggest a procedural change.

This question of different purchasing budgets is another aspect of knowing your customer and his ways, as mentioned earlier.

Keeping your ear to the ground

Self-inflicted wounds can be avoided, or the pain reduced, by one or more of the precautions described in this chapter. A general precaution is to acquire knowledge about the customer's business practices, reputation, etc. by asking around. Whenever an opportunity arises to obtain information it should be taken up. This is normally an informal process which takes place in bars, on golf courses or, for example, when your sales manager meets the sales manager of another company at a marketing seminar. 'Do you do business with See-Through Windows Ltd?' is a simple question to ask. The information which can result can be most enlightening.

We should not rely too heavily on bank references or the image of a potential customer. The *ability* to pay is usually obvious in the case of massive companies with enormous resources. The *efficiency* of their payment systems and their willingness to pay quickly is quite another matter. Sadly, some of the richest companies are also the worst payers. If that fact can be gleaned from discreet enquiries among friends or round the trade then you are forewarned.

The questions asked by a UK company providing credit insurance, on their proposal form, give a strong indication of the practices which they regard as important in knowing your customers.

The proposal form asks if the applicant investigates the creditworthiness of the customers in the following ways:

- Status reports.
  This presumably refers to the use of organisations providing financial and other information on businesses.

- Trade references.

- Bank reports.

- Establishment of credit limits as a result of previous experience.

The topics chosen by the insurers are clearly those that they consider important and, since this choice is based on long and specialised experience, indicate the steps which the businessman should take.

Are you organised for collecting money?

A small company in London had a continual problem of overdue payments. The problem was so persistent that it came to be regarded as 'normal'. That is, until times became harder and the lack of liquidity began to bite. A number of steps were taken to improve matters including earlier mailing of invoices and more use of the telephone to chase the debts. It was realised, for the first time during the review of debt-collecting methods, that there was one other fundamental weakness needing attention. This was the status of the individual responsible for credit control and his place in the organisational structure.

The clerk concerned was not only regarded as, and treated as, a junior employee, but he was also isolated from the mainstream of company activity. The low status of the individual almost inevitably meant that his job was regarded as low-status. The result was that the crucial task of ensuring that money flowed into the company was given scant attention by the managers of other functions. His isolation – in both the physical and organisational senses – meant that vetting of new business and subsequent chasing of bills was only barely a consideration in the minds of the sales force or the general management of the company. This, it was realised, had resulted in a lack of policy for collecting debts and a lack of creditworthiness guidelines for the sales force when seeking new or additional business.

After careful consideration, the clerk concerned was given the title of 'Credit Manager', was provided with training in both credit assessment and credit control and brought into the 'management team'. The result of this was a much improved cash-flow position and, after some initial antagonism, an increased appreciation by the sales force of the philosophy that a sale is not made until payment has been received.

This case-study illustrates a frequently occurring situation in growing companies. When the business is first started the proprietor, one of the partners, or some other senior person keeps an eye on debts. With the passage of time and the need to devote more effort to production and sales the chasing of debts is left more and more to the less senior person. This is often the person responsible for preparing and mailing invoices and frequently someone with no training in credit management. The end result is management neglect of the function and sales effort being expended with insufficient attention to the question 'Will we ever be paid?'

The credit management function, which will become ever more important to the health of the business as growth continues, must be kept at the centre of activity. Ideally the organisational structure will allow for the following:

- The Credit Manager will have sufficient status to influence sales planning; i.e. he will be a member of the management team.

- Pricing, invoicing and credit control will all be centred in one area.

- Sales policy will be subject to and influenced by considerations of credit control.

- There will be a close link between the sales manager and the credit manager both for the setting of policy and also to ensure that day-to-day activities include the effective collection of money. For example, using the opportunity for a salesman to ask for payment on his next call on a slow paying customer. A friendly word with the purchasing officer can work wonders – but the credit manager needs to be in a position to make it happen.

A warning to small businesses

The sole trader and the very small business run by four or five people will not have this organisational problem. Such people are normally only too well aware of what is going on and are close to *all* the action. However, as we have seen, as a business grows, debt collection tends to be one of the areas subject to neglect. The point at which this is reached is not far away from the sole proprietor or small group.

> A company providing design and other marketing services had grown to about 11 people when the proprietor became painfully aware of a cash-flow problem. He had been busy, successful and fully occupied with negotiations for larger contracts with important companies. His salesman was dashing about collecting orders, the chief designer hard at work at the drawing-board and sundry others occupied with various aspects of production.
> The invoicing? This had been left to a teenager with limited training and no sense of urgency.

The answer is to get the organisation right as soon as the second person joins the business. It may not actually be necessary at that point, but if the discipline has been established from the start it should persist into the future when it is essential. Even the sole proprietor needs to organise his time to ensure that cash flow receives regular attention.

A look into the (near) future

For many years a number of the larger businesses have carried on business by linking their computers. This method goes back to the 1960s and 1970s when magnetic tape was widely used. Transactions would be recorded by one company on a computer tape and the tape sent by courier to a client or supplying company. The second company would then run the tape on their own computer. This method was used to save masses of paper, postage costs and postage delays and also ensured that the records kept by both companies were identical. It became commonplace in dealings between banks and other companies in the financial world.

With the later developments in computer technology and the

reduction in unit cost of computing, opportunities have been recognised for the transmission of data on a routine basis between companies of all sizes and in many industries.

The result is the development of Electronic Data Interchange (EDI). This impressive sounding title should not mislead the managers of small and medium-sized companies into imagining that EDI 'is only for the big boys'. The time is fast approaching where inability or unwillingness to participate in EDI will effectively prevent a company from continuing in business at all. In fact this situation has already been reached in some fields of business with companies refusing to do business (e.g. with suppliers) except via EDI.

It is vitally important therefore to know what EDI is, how it works and the action necessary to take advantage of it.

What is EDI?

Essentially, EDI is a means of doing business without paper. Instead of typing out an invoice (or producing one by means of a computer) and sending it through the post, the 'invoice' is prepared on or generated by a computer and sent down a telephone line to the customer's computer.

The customer's computer can then update the purchase ledger and schedule the 'invoice' for payment. There will be no postal delays, much reduced chance of the invoice going astray, no paper and no excuse along the lines of 'We have not received your invoice'. Other types of error which can occur when paper is used, or can be said to have occurred in order to provide an excuse for delaying payment, are virtually eliminated when using EDI. The computers will match the various transactions used in a sales/delivery situation. Invoices, goods received notes, delivery notes and purchase orders can be compared and checked and the whole picture will be available to *both* supplier and buyer and available to be seen on a computer screen at the touch of a button. In addition, the computer can be programmed to detect any errors such as in discount calculations and only permit the data to be transmitted when it is correct. A missing order number on an invoice or any other omission can be detected and corrected, so that delaying tactics dependent on errors and omissions are prevented.

The potentialities of EDI (and in some industries the existing realities) are by no means limited to sale/purchase transactions. There are already producers of goods using EDI to communicate with buyers on the design and development of products. There are existing examples of fashion retailers using the system to interrogate a supplier's computer to check the levels of stock available, and even to make alterations in colour or design of their suppliers' products.

These facilities inherent in EDI open up a wide range of options for changing the way business is done. From a cash-flow point of view it is the speeding up of transactions and improved accuracy which is the most attractive prospect.

Is EDI for you?

The answer to this question must, ultimately, be 'yes'. Whether we like it or not (and we should like it) EDI is growing very rapidly and already many companies have found that they can only do business with some major buyers if they are willing to participate in an EDI system. One organisation in the financial world goes as far as to provide its clients with computer terminals to enable their EDI system to be used.

Most of the growth of EDI in Europe has been in the automotive and retail areas but other sectors are coming along rapidly. Various industry organisations are set up and working to develop and implement EDI and typical of these is ODETTE – Organisation for Data Exchange and Teletransmission in Europe.

ODETTE is a joint venture by major car manufacturers and parts suppliers in eight European countries.

Other industrial sectors with development organisations for EDI are:

• Pharmaceuticals

- Aerospace

- Retail and distribution

- Tourism

- Chemicals

- Construction

- Banking and finance

- Shipping

- Electronics

- Insurance

– and, perhaps inevitably, Customs and Excise. The day will come when your VAT returns will be handled on a computer link, with Customs and Excise even less willing to tolerate payment delays.

A major bank is introducing an EDI service for its customers to provide an electronic trading network throughout Europe and other major organisations are expected to provide similar services for ordering, supplying, invoicing and payment.

There is no doubt that EDI will become firmly established in the 1990s as the way to do business and all companies should be prepared for it.

How to prepare for EDI

The first requirement is to find out what is going on in your industry and who is doing what. The Department of Trade and Industry (the DTI) could be the first port of call for UK businesses. The DTI can provide advice and information on EDI in most sectors of commerce and industry via their VANGUARD service.

There is in addition a steady flow of conferences, seminars and published articles on EDI and a growing number of industry user groups from which information can be obtained.

There are also some specialist consultants who can (at a price) give you advice and guidance.

Having found out what is available and developing, an assessment can be made of what you should do.

The following are some of the likely steps to be taken:

- Arrange for one or two senior people to attend courses or seminars to obtain a good basic knowledge of the techniques.

- Contact both suppliers and customers to find out what they are doing and/or their future plans.

- Join and take part in any industry group which is preparing for or developing EDI.

- Assess the effect on your company in terms of your internal systems, staffing and staff training.

Since EDI should be regarded as an opportunity and not a problem a lot of thought should be applied to identifying the benefits which can be gained. There should certainly be some savings in labour cost. You may not need an invoicing clerk after EDI and, since every transaction should be both faster and error free, less time will be spent overall and in detecting and correcting mistakes. Both post and telephone bills should be reduced. Postal costs will be less simply because you will not be mailing your invoices. Telephone bills will go down despite the fact that the computers will use telephone lines to 'talk to each other'. The computers will do in seconds what human beings will take minutes to do. Imagine the situation when human beings are involved:

CUSTOMER:
Good morning, Fred, how are you?

SUPPLIER:
Fine thanks, George. Did you get the two packets of Floggo I sent last night?

CUSTOMER:
Hold on Fred I'll just check with . . .

(five minutes later)

CUSTOMER:
I have another order for you.

SUPPLIER:
Great, hang on while I get my order pad . . . Okay, what can I send you?

CUSTOMER:
Right, six bags of supergrade and . . .

SUPPLIER:
Hold on George, do you want the blue Supergrade or the yellow Supergrade?

. . . and so on, and so on.

In a well-designed EDI system much of this toing and froing would not be necessary and what is necessary would be accomplished in a few seconds.

Another specific subject to consider is the syntax which must be used in an EDI system. This is the set of rules to be adhered to between partners on the system to ensure that everything is standardised and all messages are comprehensible. Standards have already been developed by various bodies and the three main ones in the UK are ODETTE, EDIFACT and TRADE-CONS.

TRADECONS was first developed and published in 1982 by the Article Numbering Association and amounts to the UK industry standard. Numbers have been selected to represent and identify various products and codes for a variety of purposes such as invoices and prices.

EDIFACT is the standard for international trade covering similar needs and making possible the use of EDI links round the world. HM Customs and Excise are also taking initiatives to enhance the use of EDI, particularly in anticipation of the EC trading changes planned for 1992. A standard customs declaration message (CUSDEC) is one example of the facilities being developed.

Importers and Exporters can obtain information on these developments from HM Customs and Excise.

What about the cost?

Costs of both hardware and software are falling and an investment of around £2000 should be enough to enter an EDI scheme. Training, which is not especially demanding, can often be acquired free of charge from organisations offering EDI services. There is one cost aspect to be carefully considered and that is the type of communication line which is chosen. Leased, private lines complete with modem can be costly. They should only be considered when dealing with a customer placing so many orders that the lease cost is less than the cost of transmissions via the public network. The breakeven point needs to be worked out in advance and volumes of traffic monitored in order to be in a position to judge when a leased line is worth having.

It is fortunate for small to medium businesses that costs are reasonable in view of the major companies who are turning more and more to EDI. The costs begin to look trivial when set in the context that more than half *The Times* 100 companies use EDI, when Marks & Spencer are reported to do about 95 per cent of its buying by EDI (*Daily Telegraph*, 13 November 1989), and with companies like Ford and General Motors insisting on EDI.

EDI is growing fast – be ready for it and use it to improve your cash flow.

Avoiding self-inflicted wounds: Key Points

1. Remember that the process of avoiding payment delays starts in your office. Don't inflict unnecessary wounds on yourself.

2. Identify the delays which can be built into your internal procedures and do something about them.

3. Get to know how your customers operate and adjust your own methods accordingly.

4. Negotiate and confirm the cash and time limits.

5. Get your invoices right – first time. Take steps to avoid inaccuracies in price calculation, product description, order number, etc.
   Avoid omissions of identifying data.

6. Weigh up the pros and cons of offering a discount for prompt payment. Take care with charging interest for overdue accounts – legal advice is desirable.

7. Remember that small bills are often paid faster than large ones. Avoid accumulating bills in the interest of saving paperwork.

8. Do all you can to check the financial health of your existing and potential customers. This is an ongoing process and should not be limited to the time when you receive your first order from a new customer.

9. Consider the organisational position, status and influence of the person responsible for your credit management and debt collecting. Is the importance of sensible credit-giving taken into account before orders are accepted?
   Are sales people working with the credit management function?

10. Electronic Data Interchange is the system of the future. If you are not already involved in it take action to find out *now* what is happening in your industry. EDI can save you money and improve your cash flow, but if you are not ready for it you could lose customers who insist on using it.

5

THE DEBT COLLECTING PROCESS – CHASING THE MONEY

- Which debts to go for
- The necessary preparation
- Sending a letter
- The letter series
- The telephone call
- A matter of negotiation
- Face-to-face meetings
- Starting promptly and maintaining the pressure
- Chasing the money: Key Points

THIS chapter deals with the 'post-delay' phase. In other words, what to do if a delay in payment does occur – despite all the precautions that you have taken.

A successful approach to an errant customer depends on adopting a positive attitude based on skill and preparation. Some careful thought is required, including consideration of whether or not, at this time, to chase the debt at all.

Which debts to go for

A standard part of all accounting packages designed for use on a computer is an aged-debtor listing. This listing, which is often prepared manually by companies not using a computer, lists the outstanding debtors within 'age of debt categories' as illustrated in Figure 2.

customer	90 days +	60 days +	30 days +	current
Bloggs	100.00	50.00	250.04	120.00
Snooks	–	3900.60	1000.00	625.00
ACME	990.00	500.00	700.20	293.40
Smith	–	–	2020.15	1000.00
Brown	–	26.77	405.10	388.20
Jones	56.65	40.00	200.00	–

Figure 2: Aged debtors list

Such a listing can be most valuable, since it shows who owes what and for how long and also provides a check on money which, hopefully, will be received in due course. In short, it is part of the cash-flow forecasting scene. The routine production of the list also helps to avoid long outstanding debts being overlooked or even forgotten altogether.

Age or amount?

However, to get the best out of the aged debtors list a knee-jerk reaction, often entrenched in a hallowed, traditional procedure laid down by the company founder 50 years ago, places much emphasis on age and little on amount.

In the (fictitious) example given in Figure 2, Bloggs, ACME and Jones are, at first glance, the most serious problems. They all have debts outstanding for more than 90 days and it might be felt that the right thing to do is to clobber them with a stern warning of legal action. This will take time and effort which, for the sake of £100 in Bloggs's case and £56.65 in Jones's case, will be relatively unrewarding. ACME are more important in terms of value and should receive some attention, but the real target for attention is Snooks. Although this customer has no debts exceeding 90 days in age, they now owe a total of £5525.60 of which 89% is more than 30 days overdue.

Snooks then should be the number one target, not least to prevent them from going into the 90+ day category. If prompt payment of the £3900.60 can be achieved it will represent a significant reduction of all the money owed.

It would also make sense to spend some time chasing Smith for his £2020.15 debt as this, too, is significant in cash-flow terms.

It may go against your instincts to neglect a 90-day debt, but it is the impact on cash flow which should be your guide. The cost to you of Bloggs's or Smith's debts, for example, will be far less than the cost of Snooks's, despite the age difference.

This should not be construed as an argument to ignore the small debts: they must be dealt with at some time. Rather it is an argument for allocating precious time to work which can yield the most profit.

The 80:20 rule

A principle first stated by Vilfredo Pareto, and not surprisingly known as Pareto's Principle, can be applied to debt collecting as it can to a wide range of business activities.

Pareto stated that: 'In any series of elements to be controlled, a selected small fraction in terms of number of elements almost always accounts for a large fraction in terms of effect.'

Translated into everyday English, and applied to cash flow,

this means that a small number of customers will be responsible for most of the debt problem. The principle has come to be known as the 80:20 rule and is applicable in many situations such as:

- 20% (or thereabouts) of employees are responsible for 80% (or thereabouts) of the absenteeism.

- 80% of late deliveries will be caused by 20% of suppliers.

- 80% of complaints will be received from 20% of customers.

The 80:20 rule, when applied to debt collecting, implies that since most of the problems will be caused by only a small percentage of the customers, valuable time and effort should be concentrated on this small percentage. Analysis may show that if chase-ups are primarily aimed at the few (plus special attention to the large-value invoices) the cost of doing so will be kept low but with much the same result. In other words, an expensive 'across-the-board' campaign may not be worth while.

Whether or not this is the case in your business will depend on your own circumstances, how your customers behave and how much effort is needed to chase the debts.

Incidentally, an established policy on which debts to tackle, and when, can help to prevent causing offence to a valued customer. The following real-life case illustrates the point:

A company in the financial services industry carried on regular export business with an old and valued customer. The invoiced amounts per year added up to about $200,000. There was rarely any problem with the account and relationships were good. That is, until a clerk spotted an overdue debt which had somehow slipped through the system. The clerk sent a strongly worded letter to the customer demanding instant payment – with the threat that services would be discontinued if the money was not forthcoming within seven days. The customer, who had not been aware of the debt as a result of a muddle in the accounts, was to say the least irritated. He threatened to take his business elsewhere and some fast diplomatic action was needed to restore the former good relationship. The size of the amount overdue? $108.

The necessary preparation

Collecting debts is a process which needs preparation before execution. It *may* be possible to just pick up the 'phone, complain that you have not been paid and receive a fat cheque in the post. It is far more likely that without preparing for the call you will be wasting your time.

Without preparation – which means having all the facts at your disposal – you are likely to be stymied by one or more of the responses of the following type to your call:

- Which order number are you referring to?

- Are you sure the invoice was sent to this branch?

- I am sure we paid you last week.

- You sent us a credit note which cleared our account.

- Can you give me the invoice number?

The possibilities are many and they are often genuine queries being made by a clerk who is dealing with hundreds of invoices and dozens of suppliers. He is unlikely to have your business and all the details at the forefront of his mind. Before picking up the 'phone the facts and figures should be assembled so that you can identify the transactions you are talking about and answer any reasonable queries. This at least cuts down the chances of a long and muddled discussion (argument?) which ends with your having to say that you will ring back later when you have checked your records.

Picking up the telephone is, however, normally the second stage in a process which is often better started by writing a letter. The same preparation as is necessary before phoning is needed before writing.

Checklist of things to know *before* writing or telephoning:

1. Customer's order number and date.

2. Name of the person placing the order (if known).

3. Goods ordered – quantity, type.

4. Delivery instructions.

5. Date of delivery, place of delivery.

6. Despatch note and goods received note – numbers and dates.

7. Invoice number, amount and date.

8. To whom the invoice was addressed.

Some of these items will not apply in all cases, but all the relevant items should be ticked off.

Sending a letter

A letter, subject to its contents, is less threatening than a 'phone call and gives the recipient time to think and do some checking. It is therefore more courteous and friendly to write first. Many, perhaps most of your customers will respond to a well written letter and this reduces the list of stressful telephone calls that you must make. If no reply is made to the letter then you will have a ready-made excuse to 'phone later.

Rule number one is that the letter should be a letter, not a pompously worded routine circular with 'Dear Sir' at the start and 'Yours faithfully' at the end. Dickensian expressions should be avoided, as should accounting jargon. These will make the letter sound as if it has been produced by an antique accounting machine.

So, avoid letters like this:

Dear Sirs,

We beg to remind you that your account is now overdue. We respectfully request that you put steps in hand to regularise the position at your earliest convenience.

May we take this opportunity to respectfully remind you that our terms of trade are payment in full within 30 calendar days of the date of our invoice.

Thanking you in anticipation of an early response,

we remain,
Yours faithfully,

DINGLE, DOYLE AND DANGLE

To obtain a response from the human being who will read the letter it should sound and look as if it is written by a human being and is being sent to one. The basic requirements for your letter are:

- It should, whenever possible, be sent to a named person and not just to, say, Snooks & Co. or even Accounts Department, Snooks & Co.
  A recipient will more readily react favourably to a letter with his own name on it as this makes it more personal to him.

- The letter should be typed – or word processed. A photocopy of a standard letter with the addressee's name written in by hand looks like a routine and will be treated routinely.

- A friendly and personal tone should be conveyed, using the kind of language we use in everyday conversation.

- All the necessary identifying details should be given, e.g.
  - the invoice numbers and dates
  - the amounts due and when they were due
  - sales order and contract numbers.
  This makes it easier for the person reading your letter to

check his own records. If you fail to give the information, he will have to do some extra work. The chances are that your letter will be added to a pending tray until he has both time and inclination.

- Since it is the future you are concerned about (i.e. the customer's future actions) opportunity should be given to remove any obstacles to future settlement. For example, the customer may have a problem with one of your invoices that you are unaware of. Jog him into telling you about it with an expression such as, 'Do let us know if there is any reason why you are unable to settle the account . . .'

The resulting, typed, letter might look something like this:

Dear George,

I would be grateful if you would let us have a cheque for two overdue payments.

The items concerned are:
(i) Invoice no. 123 for £1000.00 dated 1st January (Sales order no. 6789).

and

(ii) Invoice no. 161 for £800.00 dated 3rd January (Sales order no. 6788).

As you will see these amounts are now about a month overdue.

If there is any problem with either of these items please let me know before the end of this month.

Yours sincerely

The tone of the letter is friendly but businesslike and, it will be noted, contains no threats. Threats can result in some very counter-productive and emotional attitudes and will do nothing to help develop a constructive route to an acceptable conclusion. There may be a problem which the customer is wrestling with and it may be your fault: e.g. your invoice was sent to the wrong address.

Whether or not a letter is the best way to start the process of debt collecting is a matter of judgement. In cases where the relationship between supplier and customer is close and amicable a letter may not be necessary. You may judge, from your knowledge of the customer and individuals with whom you deal that a telephone call is a better way to get things moving.

The letter series

Many companies have a laid-down procedure for chase-up letters. This is a useful provision as it reduces the chance of allowing a debt to go too far before action is taken and is far better than a haphazard 'bash at it' as and when the boss has time. Depending on your circumstances, e.g. the nature of the business you are in, two or perhaps three letters can be provided for, spaced at suitable intervals. All of them should be polite – yet even so, they should be firm. They must not follow the old fashioned pattern:

- First letter: Mildly aggressive.
- Second letter: Positively threatening.
- Third letter: We'll fix you bastards now.

The following styles of chase-up letters are more likely to succeed. But avoid following any model slavishly: individual circumstances and relationships should always be taken into consideration. The main thing to remember is – keep your letters friendly but firm.

First letter

5 April 1990

Dear Mr Brown

We wish to remind you that our invoice no.1234 for £950 and dated 1 March is now overdue for payment. We would be grateful for your remittance by return.

Yours sincerely

Second letter

19 April 1990

Dear Mr Brown

We have not received a response to our letter of 5 April regarding payment of invoice no.1234 for £950. This amount is now 19 days overdue. If there is any problem relating to the order or invoice, please let us know. Otherwise we will expect payment within four days.

Yours sincerely

Third letter

23 April 1990

Dear Mr Brown

Despite our letters dated 5 April and 19 April regarding the overdue payment of invoice no.1234, we have heard nothing from you. We are concerned that our credit terms have been significantly exceeded and will be in touch with you by telephone or visit later this week, unless payment is received in the meantime.

We are unable to accept further orders from you until payment is made, and hope that we will not be put in the position of having to take stronger action.

Yours sincerely

N.B. The second paragraph of the third letter can be omitted if it is judged that personal contact will do the trick without too much difficulty.

If, say, a week or ten days has gone by with no response to your second or third letter then the time has come for a telephone call.

The telephone call

If you have done your preparation (see pages 73 and 74) and are armed with all the facts you will be in a position to control the discussion, keep it constructive and keep it friendly.

Who to speak to

The first essential is to ensure that you are talking to the right person. You may be tempted to ask for Sir Jasper Tuff-Skinner, the chairman of the group. This will not endear you to Sir Jasper or to the people you normally deal with and, since Sir Jasper will be far removed from day-to-day transactions, there is little he can do. Alternatively, there is not much joy to be had in talking to young Ted, the most junior clerk in the accounts department, as he will possibly have no idea what to do and probably no authority to do it.

The purpose of your call is to get action and it is important to target the right person. Perhaps you have no idea who to ask for and must take pot luck in the accounts department. If so, be sure you get the name and position of the person you are put through to. Using the name helps to keep the conversation friendly and personal, and knowing the position will give you a clue as to the authority the person has.

The tone to adopt

Once you have made contact speak like a human being, not a talking accounting machine. Just a few conversational words will do the trick. For example something like the following will set the right tone.

'Hello Mrs Smith we haven't spoken for ages . . .'

'Good morning, Miss Jones, we haven't spoken before, my name is . . .'

or, if you have had a number of previous contacts,

'Hello, Bill, did you have a good holiday . . . ?'

Who you are and why you are 'phoning must be established next and, resulting from your preparation, you should have all the information in front of you which is needed to help the other person focus on the transaction you want to talk about.

If the relevant facts are clearly provided, any chance of brushing you off with an unanswerable question is removed.

The reason for your call should be clearly stated, but it helps if this is put in a non-confrontational way. It is better to ask if there is any problem which is delaying payment rather than making a demand for payment. If a problem is revealed then it can be discussed and dealt with. If not, an agreement should be sought, e.g.

YOU:
'Is there any problem with this invoice, Mr Black?'

CUSTOMER:
'No, I don't think so.'

YOU:
'Good. Can we agree to a payment by next Friday . . . ?'

It should be noted that the first question invites a 'Yes' or 'No' answer. An open question can result in a long and fruitless discussion, e.g.

YOU:
'Why has this payment been held up?'

CUSTOMER:

'Our computer has been giving us a lot of trouble, and I think our chief accountant may have had a query of some sort . . .'

If a closed question is asked and there *is* a problem with the invoice (or some other reason) then the answer 'Yes' must be followed with an explanation which is much more likely to be relevant. Vague generalisations ('I think our chief accountant may have had a query of some sort') are much less likely and you are in a better position to work to agreement.

Controlling the conversation

All conversations, whether on the telephone or face to face, can be controlled by using questions.

You may for example be dealing with a garrulous person who wants to drag you into some old problem (now dead) or down a side track.

A question, combined with use of the person's name, helps you to keep matters under control.

For example:

YOU:

'Can I expect your cheque by Friday?'

CUSTOMER:

'Well, after all the trouble we had with that mis-directed delivery last year . . .'

YOU:

'Mr Green, we sorted that out to everyone's satisfaction. Is there any problem with the delivery we are talking about?'

The second question pulls the conversation back to the subject we want to deal with, and starting by using Mr Green's name greatly reduces the risk of causing offence by interrupting him. It is an interesting point that it is possible to pull up short the most loquacious speaker by using his name. Without the name the interruption is seen as such.

Whatever happens, don't allow yourself to be pulled off the subject or dragged down memory lane. At the same time it is important to stay calm, polite and friendly. However irritating the other person may be, any hint of aggression on your part will only raise the emotional level and may end up as a blazing row. These are not the conditions in which constructive agreement is reached. They are the conditions which lead to telephones being slammed down and you no better off.

You may be dealing with a nervous or worried person who may express problems. If so, be sympathetic. Coax such a person along and help them to come to the conclusion that you want. They may have an objection or complaint and will want to tell you about it.

The complaint problem

Any complaint that the customer has is valid in his eyes. It may of course be valid in yours, too. Your closed question ('Is there any problem . . .?') may have brought out the complaint and you *must* deal with it if you are to make any progress. The complaint – even if not relevant to the outstanding debt – must not be brushed aside.

The process for dealing with a complaint is as follows:

1. Listen – get the facts. If necessary, the talker can be kept on track by means of an occasional, non-challenging, question.

2. Sympathise, but don't necessarily accept that you are at fault.
   You may be quite certain that it is the customer who is at fault and somehow you must get him to see this – without loss of face. The best solution is to give him an alibi, e.g.

ANGRY CUSTOMER:
'You sent your bloody invoice to Johnson in the Purchasing Department and not to me.'

YOU:
'I can see your problem Mr Black (sympathising) and obviously I should have let you know that your Managing

Director gave us instructions to send the invoices to Mr Johnson . . .' (giving Black an 'out').

Black will realise that his MD should have told him of the new instructions, but will be happy to think that you think that you should have done so. His anger should subside and you will be able to deal with him in a constructive way.

3. Ask questions to focus on the subject you want to discuss and to draw out any other problems which may be lurking in the other person's mind, e.g.

'Are there any other problems, Mr Black?'

'Is there anything else I should make a note of?'

4. Agree a course of action.

In Black's case you might offer to write to his MD or the Purchasing Department suggesting that the original invoice should be sent to Black and a *copy* to the Purchasing Department. Whatever it may be, the action to be agreed is one which will satisfy the customer, deal with the complaint and enable you to get back to the job of sorting out the overdue money.

Concluding the call

Having reached an agreement with the customer it is prudent to end the conversation with a summary of what has been agreed. This acts as a double check to ensure that both partners have the same idea in mind. Any difference of view as to what was agreed will only act as cause for later confusion and further delay in payment.

Conclude, then, along these lines:

'Okay, Mr Black, let's just confirm what we have agreed. I will send you copies of the last two invoices. They should reach you tomorrow. You will then draw a cheque to cover both invoices and put it in the post tomorrow night . . .'

Having confirmed what is to be done, the conversation should be ended. There is no need to go over any of the details or repeat anything concerning complaints or other obstacles dealt with. Once a tricky subject has been put to bed it should be left there undisturbed. If it is mentioned unnecessarily it might lead to starting the whole discussion all over again – which wastes time, may open old wounds and may result in a different and unwelcome conclusion. Once you have reached an agreement, shut up!

The 'phone call should of course be ended with a polite 'thank you for your help', or similar, and a friendly goodbye.

Immediately after putting the 'phone down make sure you have full notes of what was agreed. These could be helpful if, at a later stage, you have to take further action.

A *matter of negotiation*

The process of obtaining money from your debtors is frequently a matter of negotiation. That is not to say that the amount owed is negotiable. Such a case *can* occur if there is a dispute over, say, the quality of the product supplied or a misunderstanding about who pays the delivery costs.

In the majority of cases the amount owed is not in dispute, but it is often the use of negotiating techniques which produce the best collection results. The first essential – already indicated in this chapter – is to avoid an adversarial situation. The best results will be achieved both immediately and in terms of future relationships if a co-operative 'mode' is sought. This is the situation in which at the end of the day neither person feels that they have 'lost'.

It may be briefly satisfying to end the conversation with the customer feeling that you have won a battle but this feeling is often illusory and is commercially counter-productive.

The aim should be to find a 'both-win' outcome and to achieve this you may have to make some concessions – which does not mean giving money away.

Making concessions

Concessions which will get results need not cost you anything. They are also easier to use if you start off the discussion by 'aiming high'. For example, you could start by asking for full payment immediately. You can then concede by, say, agreeing to one of the payments due to you being paid three days later subject to the major part being paid immediately.

There are often concessions which you can make which cost *you* little or nothing but which have considerable value to the customer. These will become apparent if, having stated your case (aiming high), you listen carefully to the response and, by using questions, draw out any difficulties the customer may have. If by making a small concession you can help him with his difficulties, you are moving nearer to a satisfactory outcome.

There is rarely any mileage to be gained by being obstinate and insisting on 'matters of principle' which in fact have little real value to you.

Concessions you might be able to make could include:

1. Payment in two or more stages, e.g. by sending you post-dated cheques along with a current cheque.

2. Reciprocal business – they will sell you a product or service so that the payments cancel out.

3. You will give a discount on *future* orders if they are paid within 30 days and the present one paid by return.

4. Provided that the present amount is paid immediately and future invoices settled within 15 days, you will waive packaging/delivery costs.

5. You will waive packaging/delivery costs providing the present amount is paid immediately and all future orders are for not less than £X in value.

The concessions will depend on what means something to your customer and the circumstances of the case. Sensitive and careful discussion with the customer is the best way to find out which concessions will work.

The other basic rules governing the effective use of concessions are:

- Make concessions slowly. Later is better than earlier. Agreeing to something too eagerly will raise the aspirations of your customer and make him think you are a push-over.

  In addition, the longer he has to wait for a concession on your part the more he will appreciate it.

- Make concessions that give nothing away. 'I'll consider it' is a concession, as is an agreement to meet to discuss new terms of business for *future* orders.

- Let the customer make the big concessions – in return for your small ones.

- Don't be afraid to say no if too much is asked for. Many people are afraid to say no when in fact a firm and *consistent* position on your part is easier for him to accept and believe in.

Assessing your 'power'

It is a basic human characteristic to underestimate the strength of our position in a negotiating situation. If someone owes you money you will be anxious about it and tempted to believe that the customer, who has your money, has the best cards in his hand. The chances are that your customer is also anxious and thinks that you have the best cards in your hand. Don't underestimate your 'power' – this will influence your attitude and can lead you to beg and whinge which is no way to get what you want.

Keep the other *person's* viewpoint in mind

Remember that you are negotiating with a person, an individual, not a company. Companies do not buy things, agree terms or pay money. These things are all done by people. It is essential that the individual you are dealing with is treated as a person and that his conscious or unconscious feelings are respected.

He will respond favourably, or otherwise, according to the way you meet his personal needs in terms of his status, his self-respect, his sense of security and so on.

There are three 'sets' of feelings which the other person will experience and which must be taken into account in your dealings with him. They are:

1. *'I am important and I want to be respected.'*

   Insisting that he must drop everything and attend to you right away will injure this feeling, as will the adoption of a superior tone. The converse is also true and much more co-operation will be obtained if the other person is treated as a VIP – even if you are dealing with the most junior clerk in the office. Perhaps *especially* if you are dealing with the most junior clerk in the office!

2. *'I want my viewpoint taken into account.'*

   It is not necessary to agree with the other person's viewpoint, but it is necessary to show that you understand it and are not disregarding it. Brushing aside the other person's viewpoint will cause offence and encourage a belligerent attitude.

3. *'What should I do?'*

   Having to make a decision – or a promise to do something – is frequently a cause of anxiety. People hesitate and will try to put off making a commitment if they have doubts or anxieties. The skilled negotiator will recognise this and adopt an encouraging approach. Bullying or hectoring will make matters worse whereas a few encouraging words can close the deal. For example:

   'If you send me the money outstanding for August then we will have the account cleared up . . .'

   'This is the only outstanding item, so let's get it out of the way . . .'

   'I can see your problem and I will have a word with your Purchasing Director to clear things up . . .'

The words used in practice will be those which come naturally to the speaker and, importantly, will be spoken in an encouraging, friendly tone of voice.

Avoid quick deals

Always take the time necessary to think the position through. Quick deals and snap decisions are dangerous, especially in response to a 'phone call. Your customer, wanting to gain more time before paying you, may spend some time thinking out a way to do so. He then telephones you with the idea and you, entirely unprepared, may be tempted to agree to it. Unless you are quite certain, don't. It is far better to say: 'I'll think about it and ring you back.' This not only gives you time to weigh up the pros and cons without pressure but also weakens the customer's assessment of his power position. You can then call back with a counter-proposal when the customer's confidence level has fallen.

These, then, are some of the negotiating techniques which can be used. They are especially helpful in face-to-face situations where the tone of voice and facial expressions have great influence.

Face-to-face meetings

Having written a letter or two and telephoned, all without response from the customer, it may now become necessary to call on him in person. There are two types of meeting, the specific and the non-specific. The specific type is the one which is arranged solely and formally to discuss a particular matter – in this case an outstanding debt. The non-specific is the type of meeting, such as a call by a salesman, which may be routine, casual or pre-arranged in which the debt question is only one of two or more subjects to be dealt with. The non-specific meeting is particularly helpful as it is less confrontational in nature.

The non-specific meeting

You may have reason to call on the customer to discuss, say, specifications for something he has ordered; packaging, delivery arrangements or whatever.

Such meetings are a useful opportunity to raise the question of overdue money and to suggest that you are given a cheque there and then.

The successful conclusion of other matters in a friendly atmosphere is conducive to obtaining a payment. The question of payment for product or services is also seen in the context of the general business scene and arrangements for the future. The implication can be that all the happily arranged future dealings are dependent on your being paid and now is a good time to bring the financial position up to date.

Salesmen should be kept aware of the indebtedness of 'their' customers and instructed to ask for payments during the course of their round calls. This can be highly effective, as salesmen will have worked to develop a rapport with the customer's employees and will be known to them. A request from a known and friendly face carries more weight than one from an unseen Accounts Department represented by letters or a voice on the telephone.

If a customer should ask you to call to discuss some non-financial matter you can always say something like, 'By the way, the July payments are overdue. Could you have a cheque ready for me to collect . . .?'

In this situation, when you are calling at the customer's request to discuss something of importance to him, it is more than usually difficult for him to refuse your request for payment.

The specific meeting

A meeting set up solely to discuss outstanding debts probably means that things are getting serious and/or there is an obstacle (such as a complaint) to be cleared away. This places great importance on thorough preparation and arriving at the meeting armed with all the facts. All relevant documents such as copy invoices, delivery notes, sales orders and so on should be taken with you.

The way in which you go about the negotiation should be governed by all the various behavioural points already covered in this chapter. In summary they are:

- Avoid aggression and threats. Be cool, calm, polite and friendly.

- Work to agreement and a satisfactory future position.

- Control the discussion by using questions. Don't be side-tracked.

- If a complaint emerges, acknowledge it, deal with it and then get back to the purpose of your visit.

- Negotiate and be prepared to make sensible concessions but don't underestimate your strength.

- Keep the other person's viewpoint in mind and show that you acknowledge it.

- Work to agreement patiently and persistently.

As the meeting proceeds make notes of what has been agreed and encourage the other person to do likewise. This reduces the chance of a later disagreement resulting from a 'misunderstanding'.

Finally, don't hesitate to ask for your money – ideally in the form of a cheque in your hand before you leave.

Starting promptly and maintaining the pressure

In the booklet 'Action Guide – Cutting your Losses', the ECGD provide some interesting statistics.

They show that, in respect to export business, losses from 'slow accounts' are as follows:

Up to 60 days old   – 10% loss

Up to 90 days old   – 15% loss
Up to 6 months old – 50% loss
Up to 1 year old   – 70% loss
2 years or over   – 90–100% loss.

In other words, the older the debt becomes, the greater the chance of a total loss.

This confirms the importance of starting your debt chasing process without delay and keeping it up. If, for example, a debt is allowed to run for 90 days before any action is taken it will, according to the ECGD figures, have a 15% chance of being non-recoverable. After 6 months the probability of total loss rises to 50%, and so on.

Chasing the money: Key Points

1. Use an aged-debtors list, but exercise discretion as to how you use it. Concentrate your time and energy on the larger debts first. Age alone is not necessarily a guide to the debts to be chased.

2. Take account of the 80:20 rule.

3. *Prepare* carefully before taking action on a debt. Preparation is needed whatever type of action you are taking – letter, telephone call or personal visit.

4. Make your letters (and telephone calls) human. Avoid Dickensian expressions and accounting jargon. Use a friendly tone and make it as easy as you can for your customer to do what you want him to do.

5. Work towards the future and a constructive approach.

6. When telephoning, control the conversation. Use the other person's name and ask questions to keep the conversation on the right track.

7. Recognise complaints, acknowledge them and deal with them before continuing with the debt collecting process.

91

8. Conclude discussions with a summary of what has been agreed.

9. Recognise that debt collecting is often a matter of negotiating and requires the use of negotiating techniques. In particular:

   • Avoid an adversarial situation.
   • Work to a 'both-win' outcome.
   • Be prepared to make concessions – especially those which cost you little or nothing but may be very valuable to the other person.
   • Don't underestimate your 'power'.
   • Keep the other person's viewpoint continually in mind.
   • Avoid quick deals.

10. Make use of non-specific meetings. They can be a good opportunity to collect some money.

11. Start your debt collecting process promptly. The longer you leave it the greater the chance of a bad debt.

6

IF ALL FAILS – WHAT THEN?

- Cutting your losses
- To sue or not to sue?
- Going to law
- Do you need a solicitor?
- Winding up
- Arbitration
- Applying for a charging order
- Debt collection agencies
- Avoid harassment – it's illegal
- Suing an overseas debtor
- If all fails – what then? Key Points

THERE may come a point when, after every effort has been made by you, you will reluctantly conclude that your customer either cannot or will not pay up.

When this point is reached you have two options open to you. You can take no further action and write off the money as a bad debt or you can take some fairly tough action such as taking the matter to court. It is likely, however, that before this final stage is reached you will consider refusing to supply any more goods or services on credit – or at all. This sanction does sometimes produce results, but normally only if your customer is heavily dependent on you. If you have a virtual monopoly of the product he needs and he can find no substitute for it then you are in a strong position. This is of course a rare situation to be in.

Cutting your losses

You may decide to refuse further supplies, not for the reason that it will make the customer pay up, but to reduce your own exposure to loss. You may judge that further business will simply result in further indebtedness and that your wisest course is to swallow your disappointment and cut your losses.

Against this it can be argued that if you stop dealing with a bad payer then communication with him will be much reduced or eliminated since he has no further need to talk to you. This will increase the difficulty of getting money out of him.

Making the decision can be tough. However, the better you know your customer the easier it is to reach a decision. If you do decide to cut off supplies then you must stick to your guns. If at any time you relent – before the debt has been cleared – you will lose all credibility and the customer will trample all over you.

To sue or not to sue?

Whether or not to take legal action can also be a tough decision. There are some people who will not pay until the court summons lands on their doormat and doing business with them is tedious, tiresome and often unprofitable. Having discovered that one of your customers is of this type it is better to serve the summons, collect the cash and drop him forever.

Don't be fooled by the chap who eventually pays up and later, with a smooth line of talk, offers you another order with promises that this time it will all be different. It will not be different and you will once again have to spend precious time and energy to nail him. The only person likely to gain will be your solicitor to whom *you* will be paying a fat fee as a result of your customer's behaviour.

Going to law

Taking the customer to court must be the last resort. It can be an expensive process in both time and money and you need to be sure that you have the backing of evidence which will stand up in court. However, if you decide to take this step what are the options open to you?

The types of court

There are four court systems in England and Wales, two of which deal with criminal matters. The two which deal with civil cases are the County Court, which deals with minor cases, and the High Court which handles more serious matters, i.e. when more than £5000 is in dispute.

Many small businesses use the County Courts to recover debts and these courts can dispose of many claims without actually holding a trial. This arises when the person being sued has no defence or offers no defence.

Very small claims (up to £500) can be dealt with by the County Court arbitration service (usually known as the Small Claims Court). This is a private and informal process where the strict rules of evidence and procedure need not apply.

In Northern Ireland, the County Courts deal with claims up to £2000 and there is an informal arbitration service available to deal with claims up to £200.

In Scotland, there is a simple Sheriff Court procedure for claims up to £1500.

N.B. The claim limits mentioned are subject to change from time to time and should be checked if legal action is being considered.

Do you need a solicitor?

The answer is almost certainly 'yes' unless you have a clear case with sound evidence to support you. If evidence exists that the goods were delivered, were in good order, accepted and (possibly) used, but the customer has refused or failed to pay, you may be able to go it alone. However you must know what you are doing and be aware of the required procedural steps.

You will need to know, for example, how to prepare the 'Particulars of Claim' which will be required by the court. Although preparation of this document does not require the use of legal jargon, there is no printed form on which it is set out so you need to know the required layout.

There must be a title and a space for a 'plaint number' and these must be correctly positioned. Two copies must be sent to the court, the paragraphs must be numbered and so on.

If you have the time and the patience to handle the claim yourself, it can be done. There are three simple booklets which can help you. They are:

'Small claims in the County Court'
'Enforcing money judgements in the County Court'
'Suing on your own'.

These booklets, which are free, can be obtained from County Court offices and Citizens' Advice Bureaux.

Another valuable source of information, which can be helpful to your business whether or not you are contemplating legal action, is *Croner's Buying and Selling Law*. This loose-leaf publication provides up-to-date and updated explanations of the legal position, rights, duties and interpretation of the relevant Acts of Parliament.

Winding up

A step which can be taken to recover money due from an unco-operative debtor is to apply, through the courts, for a winding-up order.

This procedure (covered by the Insolvency Act 1986) can lead to compulsory winding up of the debtor's business and realisation of his assets to pay creditors. On the face of it this step looks like a way to obtain money when all else has failed and there is no prospect of, or desire for, future business with the customer.

However, care should be taken as a winding-up order may not result in your getting any money. The customer may have little in the way of realisable assets and there could be other creditors in the queue. The tax man will have first call on any available money and any debenture holders may take anything left.

In addition, a winding-up order is not a legitimate means to enforce payment of a debt if the debt is genuinely in dispute. In other words if you are saying that, say, £2000 is owed to you and the customer is saying that he did not receive the goods, this difference must be settled first. There must be no doubt that you *are* owed the money before winding up can be proceeded with.

A useful source of further information on the subject is given in *Compulsory Winding up Procedure* by Steven A. Frieze (Longman).

Arbitration

In cases where the existence of a debt, or its size, is in dispute it is worth considering arbitration as a solution – and a better one than an expensive wrangle in the courts. Cases do arise where a number of factors make the situation unclear and an arbitrator can help you reach an acceptable solution, often a compromise.

Suppose for example that you despatched 20 boxes of widgets to customer X in your lorry.

Your driver parked the lorry where directed by your customer and one of the customer's employees helped him unload. The boxes of widgets were placed on a concrete ramp outside the customer's warehouse and your driver insists that he told the customer's employee that they must be moved under cover in case of rain.

Shortly after your driver left the customer's premises it did rain and four boxes of widgets were ruined.

The customer refused to pay for the damaged widgets and his employee denies that your driver gave him a warning about the rain.

It was agreed at the outset that once the goods were unloaded they were the customer's responsibility and you have a signed delivery note to prove that he took them. The customer has argued that your driver was responsible for the unloading and should have placed the boxes in a safe place.

Who is right? Sorting out the answer in the County Court will be a lengthy and probably expensive process. A good alternative could be arbitration.

How to proceed

Provided that *both* parties to a dispute agree to arbitration, an approach can be made to the Chartered Institute of Arbitrators. The Institute will then appoint an arbitrator with the appropriate knowledge of the trade or industry who will hold a 'court' in which both parties can put their case.

The arbitrator will weigh up all the facts and present his conclusion in writing.

The court is held very informally with none of the ceremony, procedural niceties or the stress of a formal court hearing.

Arbitration offers a useful way to sort out some of the 'grey area' problems which crop up from time to time and there is the added advantage that the arbitrator is likely to have considerable experience of similar problems which have arisen in your industry before. This means that he will understand what you are talking about and the significance of various aspects of the problem. Indeed the Institute of Arbitrators has special schemes in force for a wide range of business types including for example:

- Travel industry
- Oil industry
- Plastics industry
- Franchise businesses
- Finance Houses
- Insurance

A telephone call to the Institute is all that is necessary to set the process in motion.

The normal rule is that the party who is found against (the loser) pays. However, in some cases the arbitrator may order the costs to be shared.

The size of the fee generally depends on the amount of money in dispute. The arbitrator will charge his personal fee, but this may vary according to the nature and complexity of the case. Arbitrators' fees are very variable and are normally in line with those of solicitors and accountants.

Applying for a charging order

Mention has already been made of the problem of taking action in the courts when, because the debtor has no assets, you still do not get your money. There is the possibility in some cases where assets do exist of obtaining the money as a result of a Charging Order.

Courts, under section 1 of the Charging Order Act of 1979 are empowered to make an order whereby the debt owed to you can be registered against property owned by the debtor. Normally land would be the property targeted in such an action but other assets such as units held in a unit trust or stock in any organisation except a building society can be involved.

The first stage in the procedure is to make application to the court stating:

- the particulars of the debt

- details of the property to be charged

- belief that the property is owned by the debtor.

99

If the court grants the application a Charging Order *nisi* is made. This means that unless cause is shown why the Order should not be made, it will be made *absolute*.

The second stage involves the debtor being summoned to the court to present any case he may have for the order *not* to be made absolute.

Other interested parties such as a bank or building society will also be summoned to the hearing and unless the debtor is able to show either that the debt is not due *or* that he in fact has no interest in the property the Order will be made absolute.

In such an event the creditor may have to make an application for the sale of the property in order to obtain the amount due to him.

Sometimes a debtor will try to wriggle out of the Charging Order by selling the property before the charge becomes absolute and, if this is known, an injunction may have to be applied for in order to restrain him. This can be done at the time of the original application and as part of the original application.

A Charging Order can still be obtained if the property is jointly owned, e.g. by a husband and wife. The facts of ownership can, where land is involved, be ascertained by reference to the Land Registry and there are provisions in the 1979 Act for this.

It will be seen that applying for a Charging Order is a fairly complex business and ideally a good solicitor should be employed to act for you.

Debt collection agencies

Placing the problem in the hands of a firm of debt collectors is another option open to you. Some people are reluctant to try this option because of fears of the methods which might be used to 'persuade' the customer to pay up. Visions of large men with cauliflower ears and an enthusiasm for breaking arms and legs can be very off-putting to the respectable businessman.

However, in normal commercial life this image is wholly

misleading and most debt collecting agencies are highly reput-able organisations – including many firms of accountants.

The company accountants should be consulted as they may operate a debt collecting service or be able to recommend another firm that does. It is important to find out what methods are used by the debt collectors you are considering. Clearly they will, at times, be obliged to apply some pressure to the unwilling debtor and the precise nature of this pressure is something you should be aware of and be happy with. It is often the case, however, that a debtor will take more notice of a debt collecting agency than the supplier of their goods. A positive reaction to the first, polite, request to pay up frequently results simply because the debtor will realise that he is now dealing with a specialist organisation with the time, resources and persistence to pursue the debt.

The fees charged are normally a percentage of the amount of money recovered although some agencies work on a flat fee basis related to the time spent on your behalf.

Avoid harassment – it's illegal

You may be tempted to put some pressure on your debtor in a manner designed to embarrass him into paying up.

Such a course of action – not unknown as a tactic used in the past by less responsible debt collecting firms – is liable to fall foul of the Administration of Justice Act 1970. Section 4 of the Act states:

> A person commits an offence if, with the object of coercing another person to pay money claimed from the other as a debt due under contract, he – 'harasses the other with demands for payment which, in respect of their frequency or the manner or the occasion of making any such demand, or of any threat or publicity by which any demand is accompanied, are calcu-lated to subject him or members of his family or household to alarm, distress or humiliation'.

This means that telephoning your customer in the early hours of the morning or pestering his wife could be an offence. Threats to put up a notice in the golf club stating that Joe Bloggs owes you a lot of money is also likely to be regarded by the courts as harassment.

Moreover, you could be liable if a debt collection agency acting on your behalf uses methods designed to humiliate or cause distress or alarm.

You are allowed to take action which is 'reasonable and otherwise permissible in law'. What is 'reasonable' depends on the circumstances, but includes letters, writs and summonses served on the debtor by a lawyer.

Suing an overseas debtor

Suing a customer in a foreign country – possibly a country with a very different legal system – can be tricky. However, it can be made much easier by taking a simple precaution when drafting the contract on which the business will be based. The objective should be to ensure that any disputes can be settled in a court of *your* choice (the jurisdiction) and a form of law which *you* prefer.

This can be ensured by a clause in the contract along the following lines:

> Any dispute arising out of this contract will be governed by English law and referred to the High Court of Justice of England and Wales.

The existence of a clause such as this will enable you to issue a writ in an English court and to seek leave to serve it in another jurisdiction.

You will, by this means, also ensure that the dispute will be dealt with in accordance with English law and not some less predictable system ill-suited to modern commercial matters. In addition, you will avoid the danger of losing your case as a result of bribery of court officials, judges or witnesses – a widespread practice in some parts of the world.

The wording of the appropriate clause in your contract is a job for a lawyer (even if the resulting wording appears to be very simple), as the whole question of jurisdiction is a complex one. Without the right clause you could find yourself in considerable difficulty and paying vast legal fees merely to establish jurisdiction, before any action can be taken.

An example of the complications is the question of where the contract is deemed to have been made. It need not be in either your country or your customer's country! Under English law a contract is deemed to have been made:

- In the country where the telex accepting the offer is received – if the deal is done by telex. (Telephone deals are treated in the same way as telex.)

- In the country where the letter is posted if the acceptance is by letter.

If, therefore, you received a telex accepting your offer while you were travelling in America then American jurisdiction applies – even if your business is in England and your customer is in Japan. Having to conduct your case in America would not be as easy and will undoubtedly be more expensive than suing in the English courts.

Whatever the situation you will need a competent lawyer to assist you in suing an overseas debtor. Your local firm of solicitors *may* be able to handle it but you must be sure that your lawyer has specialist knowledge in the subject. Your local Chamber of Commerce or your trade association should be able to put you in touch with a lawyer of the right type.

Last, but by no means least, obtaining a judgement against a foreign individual or corporation is by no means the end of the story. The greatest difficulty is then enforcing a judgement when you have it. Although, as a result of an EC Convention, this is now easier if the debtor is resident in the EC, in many countries enforcement can be an expensive and time-consuming task. It is therefore always a good idea to try to obtain security for your claim *before* embarking on expensive litigation – for example through the ECGD (see page 34).

If all fails – what then?

1. Making the decision as to whether to regard the debt as a bad one and write it off or to take further action can be a tough one – but it must be faced. The pros and cons must be weighed up but you are better off without a customer who will not pay until you take him to court.

2. It is possible to sue without a solicitor and small claims may be dealt with on a do-it-yourself basis. Advice can be obtained from the County Courts or the Citizens Advice Bureaux.
   If in doubt – use a lawyer.

3. Don't go for a winding-up order if the debt is genuinely in dispute.

4. Consider arbitration as an alternative to action in the courts.

5. A Charging Order may be the best way to get your money if the debtor has assets such as land which he can be forced to sell.

6. Consider the use of a debt collection agency as another alternative.

7. Avoid action which might be regarded as harassment.

8. When contracting with an overseas customer, ensure that any disputes can be settled in a court of your choice and be governed by a form of law which you prefer.

═ 7 ═
FACTORING – THE ANSWER TO THE DEBT PROBLE M?

- **What is factoring?**
- **The limitations in factoring**
- **What are the benefits to you?**
- **What about the drawbacks?**
- **Factoring: Key Points**

What is factoring?

Put very simply, a factoring company will advance to you a percentage of the value of your outstanding sales invoices. This means that instead of having to wait until your customer pays up you will receive, virtually immediately, some of the cash.

There are a number of variations on this basic theme and, not surprisingly, there is a price to pay for it.

There are four main types of factoring services available. They are:

1. Invoice discounting

This is the simplest (and fastest growing) service offered by the factoring companies. It is also the cheapest.

With this system you prepare your own invoices, keep your own sales ledger and do all your own administration. You also collect all your own debts.

The factoring company advances you up to 80% of the value of your invoices which provides you with 'instant cash' to keep the business going. There is a surprisingly widespread belief that the factoring company keep for themselves the remaining 20% of the value of the invoices. This is not the case, but you will have to pay a fee. This fee varies depending on volumes and the amount of work which the factoring company must undertake. Normally the charge will be in the order of 1.5–3% *above base rate*.

There are differences in the way that factoring companies calculate their fees – some, for example, will provide the money cheaply but bill you for 'handling charges'.

2. Recourse factoring

In this version the factoring company keeps your sales ledger for you and collects all the debts. However, the client company remains responsible for any bad debts and this type of factoring should not be mistaken for a protection against loss if your customer goes to the wall.

Perhaps for this reason recourse factoring is said to be most popular with companies doing business with soundly financed organisations or a wide range of customers who purchase small value goods and services, i.e. each debt is small and if things go sour the loss will not be very damaging.

3. Non-recourse factoring

With this form of factoring the client company *is* protected against bad debts. The factoring company takes on this risk – at a price.

The factoring company will insist on vetting the client's customers for creditworthiness and may choose to reject those it considers to be a bad risk. This, in a sense, reduces the value of the non-recourse service since it limits your freedom to trade with all and sundry and still have protection against a bad debt.

However, the fact that the factoring company turns down a prospective customer on the grounds of financial shakiness provides the protection against worry and hassle which ideally you should have gained as a result of your own enquiries. There is little joy in doing business with a company which goes bust, even if you are protected against the bad debts which result. Forward planning and development of your business needs to be against a background of continual and long-term stability, with the same customers placing regular orders. Without this stability, cash-flow forecasting becomes cash-flow guessing – a situation fraught with dangers and anxieties.

You can of course decide to continue with business which the factoring company has rejected, but you will be taking a risk and you will have been warned.

4. Export factoring

This service normally offers 100% cover against bad debts with up to 80% advance of money against invoices.

The limitations in factoring

Some limitations have already been mentioned such as the possible rejection of unattractive customers in the non-recourse schemes.

There are other limitations to be aware of, such as:

● It is unlikely that a factoring company will take on your business if your annual turnover is less than £100,000 per year. Although some factoring companies claim to help and support small businesses they do not all help and support *very* small businesses. However, competition in factoring is hotting up and more flexibility may become apparent as more factoring companies appear on the scene. Indeed, at least one UK factoring company claims that it is willing to consider start-up and management buy-out situations and it is worth the trouble for small businesses to make enquiries.

● Factoring companies are most unlikely to advance money against invoices which are already overdue for payment when the agreement starts. This is entirely understandable but in reality it effectively prevents the business which is already in trouble from getting out of it simply by signing a factoring agreement and receiving an immediate injection of badly needed cash.

● Some factoring companies insist on a substantial spread of debtors. It may be a requirement that no one customer accounts for more than say 25% of total business. Any company in such a position is in any case vulnerable, but it is often a long hard struggle to widen the customer base to avoid such dependence on one source of income. In the meantime the factoring companies may not be willing to do business with you.

● A minimum average invoice value may be insisted on by the factoring company. It is unlikely that an average less than about £100 will be acceptable. This may appear odd at first sight as it might be argued that the small values represent low loss levels in the event of a bad debt occurring. The reason is an economic one. It costs as much to record and process a £50 sale as it does for a £50,000 sale and it can become unprofitable for a factoring company to deal with a multitude of small transactions.

What are the benefits to you?

Direct financial benefits

The extent to which factoring is of benefit to a company depends primarily, and in a purely financial sense, on how much working capital is tied up in outstanding debts. A figure of around 40% is not uncommon and in the case of purely service companies who do not hold stocks could be much higher.

The cost of this outstanding debt can be high and can probably be measured by the cost of any bank overdraft or loan necessary to support the situation. If the outstandings can in effect be reduced by factoring to around 8%, the impact on the cost of bank borrowing can be readily calculated. This saving must be set against the fees to be paid to the factoring company, but there is a fair chance that you will find a factoring deal cost-effective.

The number of companies using factoring services has grown rapidly during the 1980s and this indicates the financial advantages. The Association of British Factors, which represents ten of the larger factoring companies, claimed that its members had in excess of 6000 clients in 1988 – a rise of 14% over the previous year.

Spin-off benefits

However, the benefits of factoring your invoices are not limited to reducing the cost of financing your customers' debts. There are wider and often far-reaching spin-offs to be taken into account. These benefits include:

- The improvement in cash-flow means that optimum stock levels can be maintained. It may also be possible to put pressure on *your* supplier to offer better deals (e.g. discounts) by virtue of your ability to pay promptly.

- You will be better enabled to take on larger orders knowing that you will have the money to cope with them.

- Depending on the scheme arranged with the factoring company you can save on administration costs. If the factoring company handles your sales ledger, you will not have to employ your own sales ledger clerk – who may be difficult to find in the first place and require training and constant supervision when you have found him. There can also be savings in office space requirements, postage cost, telephone bills and so on.

- More management time is available for running other aspects of the business. Attention can be paid to production (and productivity), sales, purchasing and development without time-consuming chasing of debts burning up your energies.

- There is a reduced chance of losing customers as a result of relationships being strained by repeated nagging for prompt payment.

- The financing of the business is closely related to its volume of activity. The flow of money resulting from factoring is directly governed by the value of the invoices prepared. This is a fundamentally important point when comparing financing via factoring with bank loans and overdrafts.

  It is common practice for branch bank managers to base their decision on balance sheets and past performance. Balance sheets are one of the least useful and informative means to assess the future potential of a business: not only are they concerned entirely with history, but they give a one-off 'snapshot' of the state of a business at a specific time.

  Despite the limitations of the balance sheet the cautious branch manager (who in any case has limited powers delegated by head office) will use it to judge whether he is prepared to grant a bigger overdraft. You, on the other hand, will be aware of future sales opportunities for which you need the finance. Factoring can provide this finance when your bank manager will not. This is perhaps most marked when the factoring company is not owned by one of the banks. Independent factoring companies are not constrained by the usual banking criteria and tend to take a 'trading view' of their clients' businesses. This enables the independents better to tailor their arrangements with clients individually.

- Seasonal fluctuations in sales are a problem for some businesses. The famine period will need support as the overheads of rent, rates, insurances and the like will still be there. Factoring at least reduces the size of the seasonal problem by avoiding the additional burden of money being tied up in debts at a time when it may be desperately needed.

What about the drawbacks?

Although factoring has been a flourishing business in many countries throughout the eighties (particularly in the USA, the UK and Italy) growth has been hampered by some real or imagined drawbacks.

Client resistance has been based on the following notions:

Fear of what the customer will think

Businessmen have expressed the fear that customers will assume that they are in financial difficulties if a factor is involved. This worry, which will in any case diminish as factoring grows and becomes more widely understood, can be taken care of in two ways.

Firstly, the arrangement can be entirely confidential so that your customer does not know that a factor is involved. Secondly, if your customer is to know that a factor is involved he can be sent an explanation by letter which points out the reasons. The reasons of course will be constructive and forward-looking and designed to remove any doubts. A good factoring company will provide help in this respect and will be well aware of client/customer sensitivities.

Factoring companies are 'lenders of last-resort'

In other words, they back unsound businesses and are somehow not respectable. This is an emotional and inaccurate judgement of an industry which includes some very prestigious names. There is also a misconception that factoring is a young, untried business. Although growth in factoring has been most marked in recent years it has, in fact, a long history. The US textile trade was using factoring in the nineteenth century, although it is fair to say that European countries did not import the idea until the 1960s.

The 'I have failed' syndrome

One young entrepreneur expressed his feelings as follows: 'I have worked hard to build this business from nothing. It is a point of pride with me that I did it all myself and using a factor would be an admission of failure.' This is also an emotional reaction which does not stand up to serious scrutiny. If factoring can make your business stronger, then using it is no sign of failure – rather the reverse.

Heavy-handed debt collection methods will be used

It is contrary to the interests of factoring companies to damage or destroy the businesses of their clients by heavy-handed methods. The industry also recognises that subtlety pays off in most cases and will adopt a sophisticated approach to debt collection.

The methods which a factoring company will use can and should be clarified before entering into the factoring agreement so that you are not working in the dark and subject to a sudden shock. If the factor does not satisfy you on this point there are others to choose from. The fact is that there is no discernible history of bad practice and if a problem does arise with a particular customer it is normally possible to agree with the factoring company how the situation will be handled.

Factoring is an option which should be seriously considered by any business with a cash-flow problem – which is probably the majority! It is desirable to contact three or four factoring companies to compare their services and costs before making a choice.

Don't be put off if one of the larger ones turns you down. Attitudes vary and there is almost certain to be a competitor who will offer you a fair deal.

Factoring: Key Points

1. There are four main types of factoring service available. This provides a choice of service level and cost.
2. There are some limitations to factoring (which should be clearly understood before entering into a factoring agreement). In particular a factoring company will not take on invoices which are already overdue – factoring is unlikely to be a way to save a business which is already in serious trouble.

3. Factoring offers a number of potential benefits including:

   - Improved cash-flow with less working capital tied up in debts. This can result in more economic stock holding and more cost-effective purchasing.
   - Reduced cost of financing debts.
   - Reduced payroll and administration costs.
   - More management time available for sales and production.
   - The finance of the business is related to its volume of activity rather than a bank manager's opinion of your (historical) balance sheet.

4. There have been (and still are) misconceptions about factoring, e.g. that customers will think you are about to go bust. These misconceptions should be seen as such.

Appendix 1

GETTING A BETTER DEAL FROM THE BANK

WITH business expanding a growth in outstanding debts is almost inevitable. It is just at this time that additional financing is likely to be required and, even if you are factoring your invoices, another trip to the bank manager may be necessary.

If you are successful in obtaining the facilities needed you will be taking up yet another burden of expense – the charges that the bank manager will make.

It is important to ensure that these charges are as low as you can get.

Interest rates

The fact is that the charges, within limits, are negotiable and it is not necessary to accept, docilely, the proposed cost of borrowing the money. However busy you may be it is worth taking the time to check the basis of your banking arrangements – and don't be afraid to challenge the bank manager. It appears that managers will often charge 'what the traffic will bear' – in other words, what they think they can get away with. This means that you could be paying one per cent above base rate, or two per cent, or five per cent or even more. The difference can be substantial and makes the servicing of your debts a greater problem.

Bank managers are reluctant to admit that they have room for manoeuvre or that they are actually worried that you will change banks. Closing the account is not something the manager will find comfortable and you could have more negotiating power than you may think.

Check also, and challenge, the arrangement fees that banks are fond of, and ask for a change in the agreements which were reached when interest rates were higher than at the present time or when your business was smaller.

Bank charges

Another potentially fruitful area are charges for transactions i.e. payments to and withdrawals from your company account. Some banks publish the charge that they make for each transaction, some do not. You should at least know what the charge is and compare it with the charges made by competitor banks. This is especially necessary if you are exporting and paying in foreign currency cheques. These transactions can involve an 'enrolment fee' and a service charge for each cheque. Banks can be coy about how much the service charge will be at varying levels of turnover and can soak up much of the profit margin if your business involves multiple low value sales.

> A small publisher mailing to overseas customers was quoted a charge of £3 per cheque paid in. Since the average cheque value was only £2.75 using the bank concerned was a sure route to bankruptcy. After some enquiry the company concerned found a satisfactory service elsewhere.

Clearly it pays to shop around.

Using a Building Society

One way to reduce costs which should appeal to small businesses is to use a Building Society account as a 'halfway house'. If all receipts are paid into a Building Society cheque account they will not be subject to charges and will accumulate interest. When the time comes to pay your own suppliers' bills *one*

Building Society cheque can be paid into your bank account to provide the necessary funds. This could mean that instead of paying say, 50 transaction charges you will pay only one. In addition you will have earned some interest in the Building Society account.

Above all, when dealing with your bank manager don't believe him when he says (with apparent sadness and sympathy), 'I'm sorry, Mr Snooks, there is nothing I can do to help you.' There *is* something he can do and he will do it if you use some muscle. If not, try another branch or another bank.

Appendix 2

BREAKEVEN POINT

THE concept of breakeven point is simple and valuable but only too frequently neglected in business.

Breakeven point calculations should be made by any business which wishes to have a complete control of its financial affairs and a clear understanding of what is going on.

The calculation itself is best given by a simple example such as this:

Suppose a company is making coffee tables. The company will have certain fixed costs which it must pay regardless of how many tables are made. Let us assume that they are as in the following illustration:

Fixed Costs (per month)	£
Workshop rent and rates	500
Insurances	10
Machinery lease payments	50
Labour	1000
TOTAL:	1560 per month

Further costs will be incurred when some coffee tables are made. These costs are variable and depend on how many tables are made. For example, the variable cost in respect of one table might be:

Variable Cost	£
Timber	10.00
Varnish and polish	1.00
Transport	3.00
Electricity, sandpaper, etc.	1.00
TOTAL:	15.00

Let us now suppose that the tables can be sold at £40 each. The production volume required to make a profit can be seen from the table below:

Number of Tables	Fixed Cost	Variable Cost	Total Cost	Sales Revenue: £s	Result: £s
1	1560	15	1575	40	Loss of 1535
10	1560	150	1710	400	Loss of 1310
50	1560	750	2310	2000	Loss of 310
100	1560	1500	3060	4000	Profit of 940

It will be seen that the changeover from loss to profit lies somewhere between 50 and 100 tables made and sold. The actual breakeven point is 63 (in fact a profit of £15 would be made at this point but a small loss would result at the 62 table level).

The value of this calculation in terms of credit control is that it shows not only how many tables must be made each month to make a profit, but also the amount of variable cost to be met. This, added to the fixed costs, shows how much money must flow into the business, on average, each month in order to survive. This in turn, taking into account the various forms of working capital, indicates the maximum outstanding debt that the business can sustain.

In other words, the breakeven point when calculated gives you a feel for the volumes you must make, the financial resources required and how much credit you can give your customers.

The calculation can also be used to demonstrate the effect of charging higher prices or cutting costs. Both of these will change the breakeven point.

The concept of breakeven can be illustrated graphically – as shown in Figure 3.

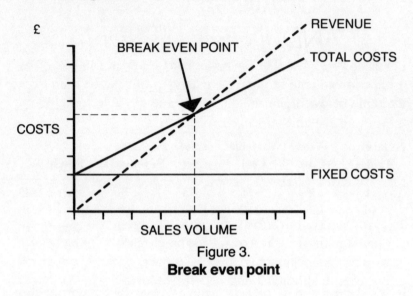

Figure 3.
Break even point

Appendix 3

SOURCES OF HELP AND INFORMATION

SOME of the organisations which may be able to help you with advice and information include:

1. The British Institute of Management
Cottingham Road, Corby, Northamptonshire NN17 1TT Tel: 0536 204222

The BIM carries out surveys and studies from time to time on a variety of management topics – including Credit Management. The BIM Management Survey Report No. 52 on credit management, although published some years ago (1981), makes interesting reading. Among other useful findings the BIM reported that telephone calls and statements were the most effective means of collection of money in the textile industry and telephone calls plus withholding supplies in the electronics industry.

2. The Association of Independent Businesses
133 Copeland Road, London SE15 3SP Tel: 071–277 5158

The AIB claims to be the only organisation which 'uniquely represents the interests of independent businesses'. The Association works to influence government ministers, the European Parliament, banks, local authorities and other institutions on behalf of its members.

Advice is provided on a wide range of subjects including debt servicing and debt collection.

A regular newsletter is also published covering a variety of topics of interest to the small business.

121

One of the Association's stated aims for the future is 'prompt debt payment by large companies'.

Membership fees are reasonable and based on the number of employees.

3. The Institute of Credit Management
Easton House, Easton on the Hill, Stamford, Lincolnshire, PE9 3NH Tel: 0780 56777

The Institute is the professional body for Credit Managers. It publishes a monthly journal dedicated to credit management topics which provides news on legislation, interpretation of the law and other relevant topics.

Seminars are run by ICM at various locations round the country on such topics as:

• Basics of Credit Control

• Successful Negotiation for Credit Managers

• Law for the Credit Manager.

4. London Chamber of Commerce
69 Cannon Street, London EC4N 5AB Tel: 071–248 4444

The Chamber provides advice on a wide range of subjects – not least by means of talks and seminars. It also publishes a journal covering many topics of interest to businesses.

5. Department of Trade and Industry
1 Victoria Street, London SW1H 0ET Tel: 071–215 7877

The DTI can be particularly helpful to exporters and would-be exporters. Specialists are employed with detailed knowledge of various parts of the world and how business is conducted in them.

6. The Chartered Institute of Arbitrators
75 Cannon Street, London EC4N 5BH Tel: 071–236 8761

The secretary will provide you with details of the work of the Institute and its members.

The Institute may have an arbitration scheme in existence for your particular trade or industry.

7. The Association of British Factors
   Information Office, 24–28 Bloomsbury Way, London WC1A 2PX Tel: 071–831 4268

The ABF represents the larger factoring companies, many of which are owned by major banks.

It is unlikely that any number of the ABV would be interested in a turnover of less than £100,000 p.a.

8. Association of Invoice Factors
   Jordon House, 47 Brunswick Place, London N1 6EE

Information can be obtained by writing to the above address or by telephoning 0232 (Belfast) 324522.

9. Small Business Research Trust
   School of Management, Open University, 1 Cofferidge Close, Stony Stratford, Milton Keynes, MK11 1BY

The SBRT carry out surveys among small firms on business topics. The surveys, which began in 1983, are published quarterly and available for a fee of £45 p.a.

Useful reading, in addition to the publications of the organisations already mentioned, includes:

Croner's Buying and Selling Law (Croner Publications Ltd)

Arbitration (Sweet & Maxwell)

Compulsory Winding up Procedure by Steven A. Frieze (Longman)

Business Credit a bi-monthly journal '. . . designed to assist in the efficient use of credit and management of credit by business undertakings large and small'. This journal is obtainable from the subscription office at 46 Bridge Street, Godalming, Surrey, GU7 1HH

A very readable book covering the control of working capital is *So you think you are in BUSINESS?* published by Video Arts, Dunbarton House, 68 Oxford Street, London W1N 9LA.

The major accountancy journals have useful and relevant articles on credit management from time to time. One or more of the following might be added to your regular reading list: *Accountancy*, *Accountancy Age*, *Management Accounting*.

INDEX

Business Books for Successful Managers

PIATKUS BUSINESS BOOKS have been created for people like you, busy executives and managers who need expert knowledge readily available in a clear and easy-to-follow format. All the books are written by specialists in their field. They will help you improve your skills quickly and effortlessly in the workplace and on a personal level.

Each book is packed with ideas and good advice which can be put into practice immediately. Titles include:

The Best Person for the Job, Malcolm Bird

The Complete Time Management System, Christian H. Godefroy and John Clark

How to Collect the Money You are Owed, Malcolm Bird

How to Develop and Profit from Your Creative Powers, Michael LeBoeuf

How to Win Customers and Keep Them for Life, Michael LeBoeuf

Leadership Skills for Every Manager, Jim Clemmer and Art McNeil

Powerspeak: the Complete Guide to Public Speaking and Communication, Dorothy Leeds

Smart Questions for Successful Managers, Dorothy Leeds

The Strategy of Meetings, George David Kieffer

Your Memory, Kenneth L. Higbee

You too can benefit from expert advice. Just look out for our distinctive Piatkus silver business book jackets in the shops. For a free brochure with further information on our complete range of business titles, please write to:

Business Books Department
Piatkus Books
5 Windmill Street
London, W1P 1HF

PIATKUS